Subodh Gupta *Common Man*

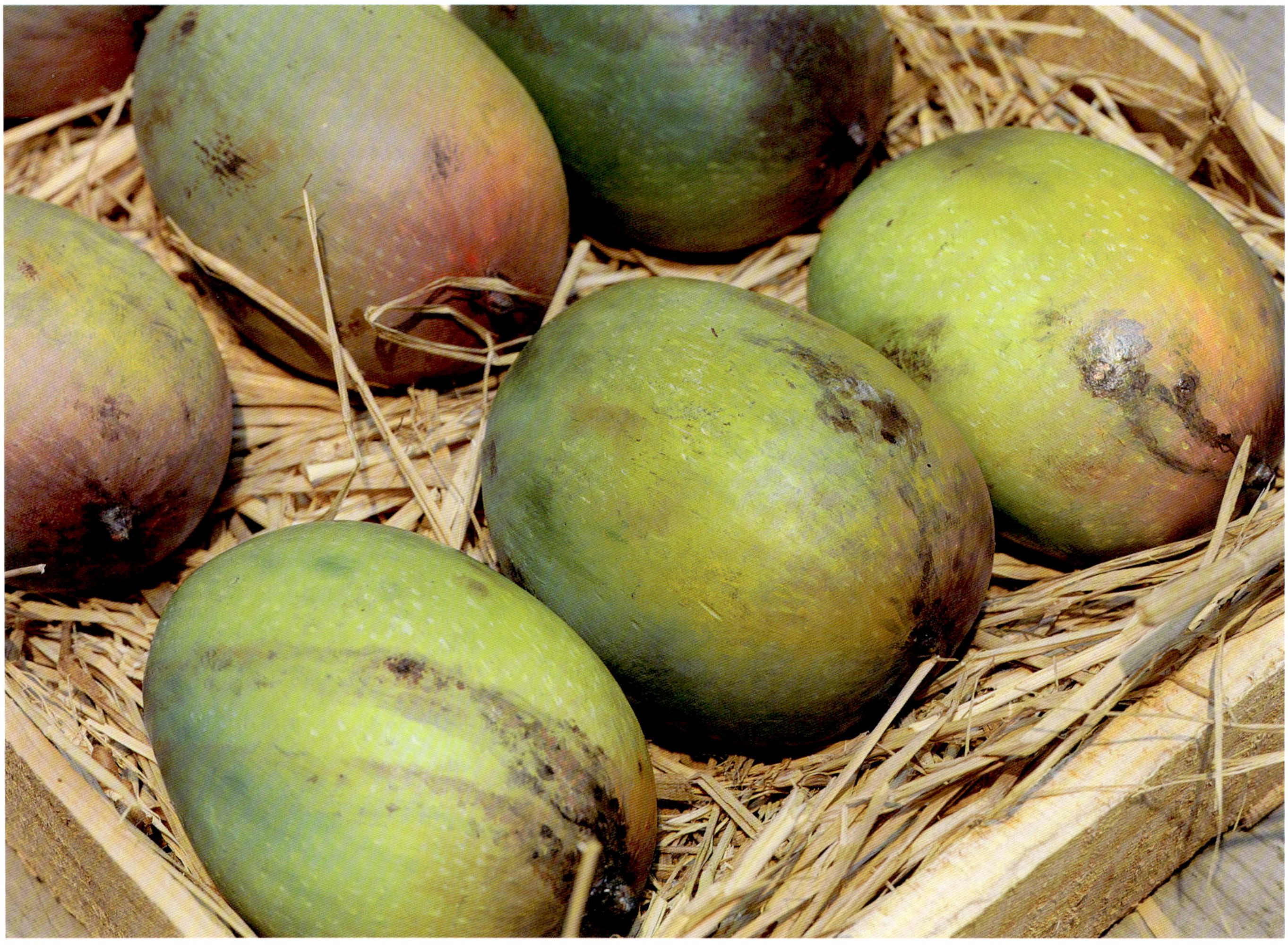

Subodh Gupta

Common Man
आम आदमी

JRP|Ringier

Contents

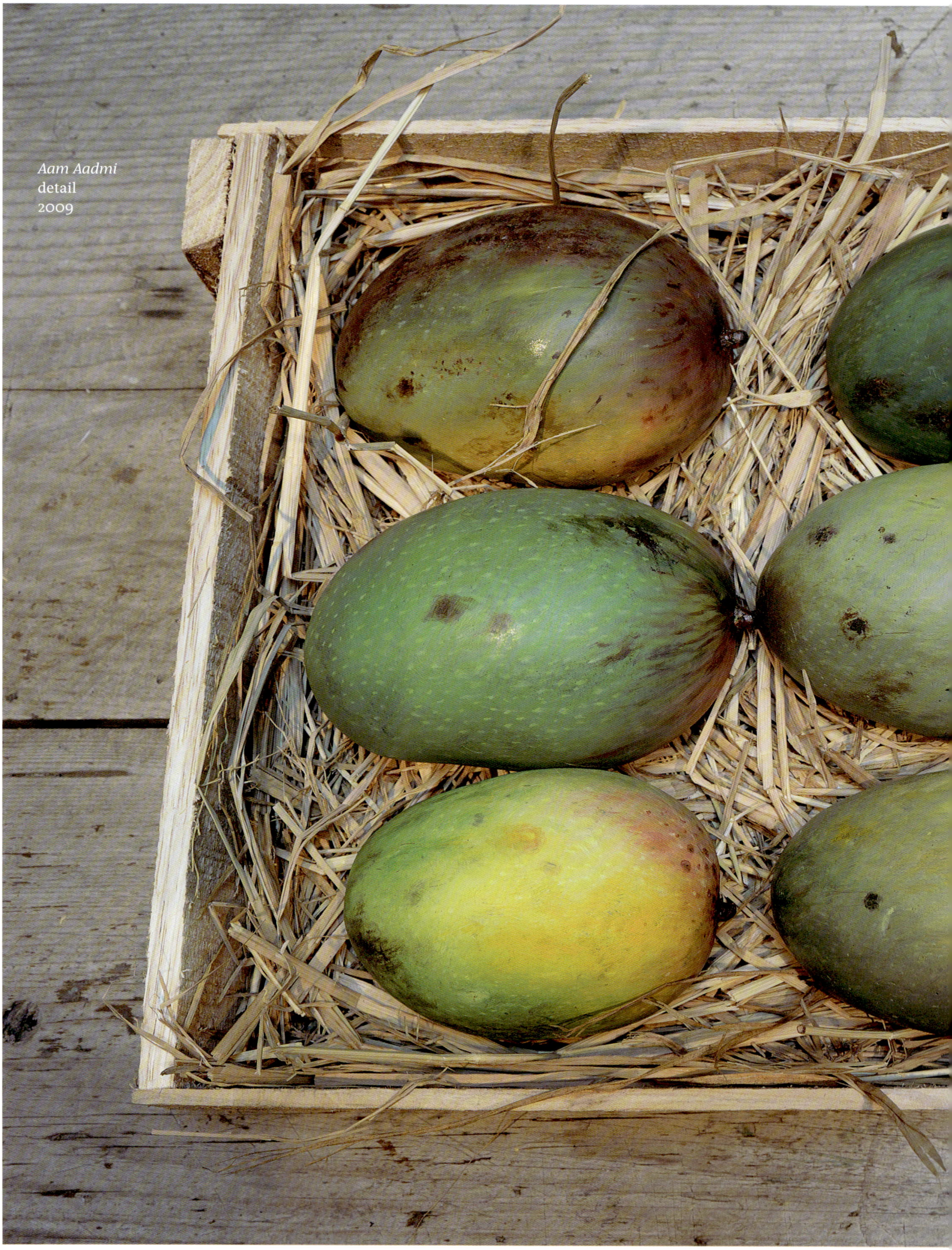

Aam Aadmi
detail
2009

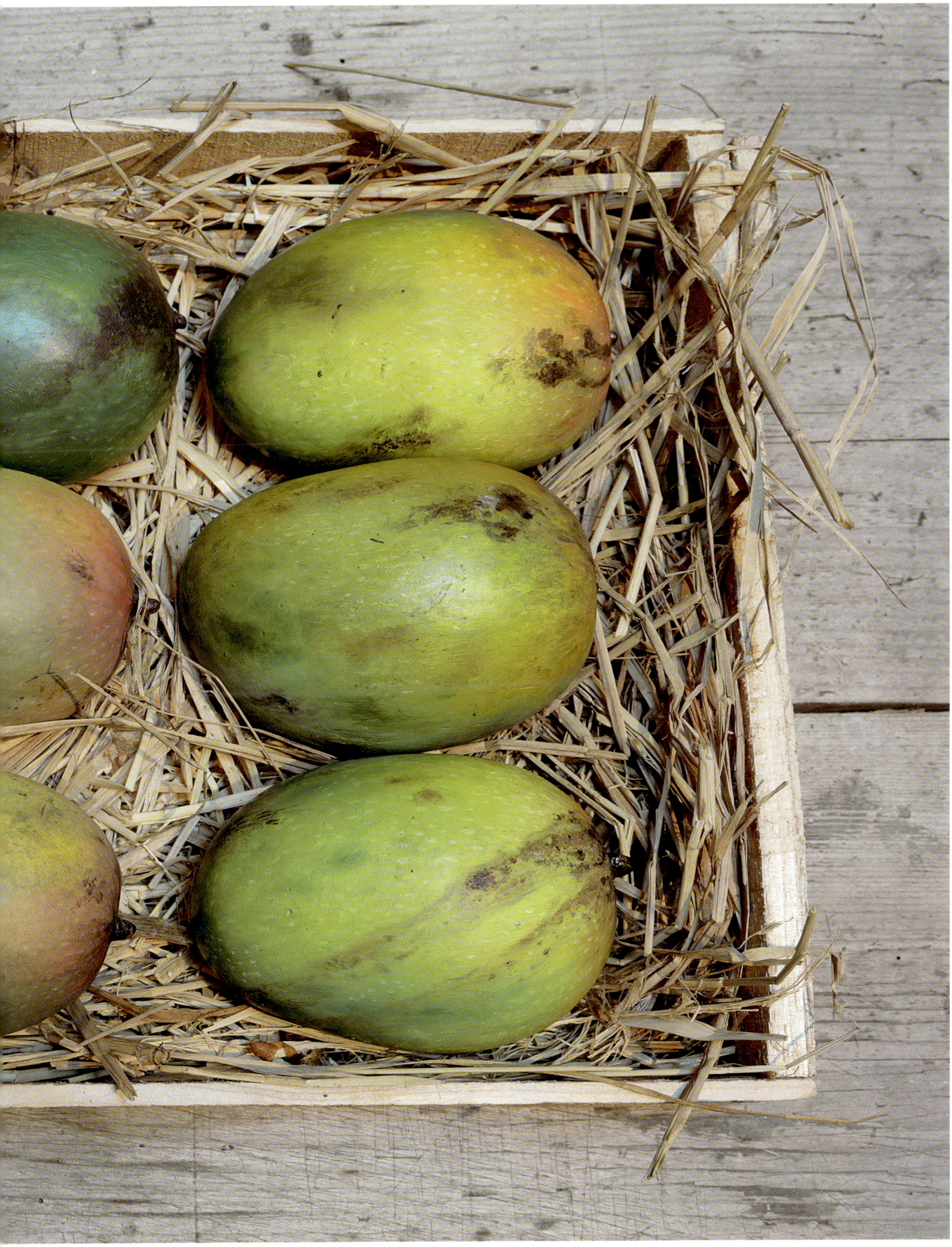

Studio view, New Delhi

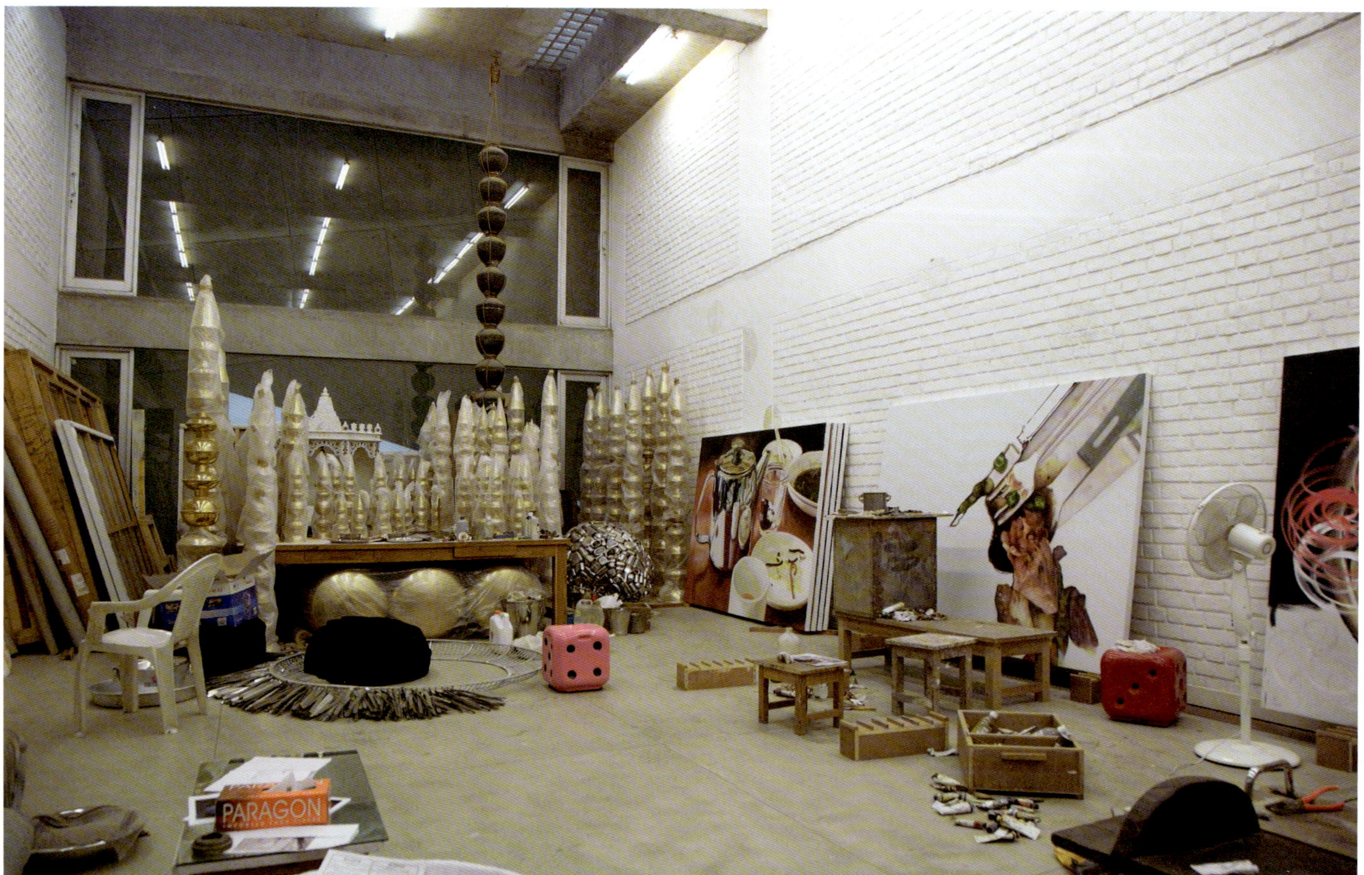

Subodh Gupta and Hans Ulrich Obrist in conversation

New Delhi, June 2009

HANS ULRICH OBRIST: Last time I visited you in this neighbourhood you had a rather small space. Now you've got your own big space. I am very interested in this idea that artists build their own studios. Joan Miró had his studio built by a great Spanish modernist architect called Josep Lluís Sert. Obviously, when artists build their own studios it has a lot to do with light.

SUBODH GUPTA: It was a dream to have my own studio.

HANS ULRICH OBRIST: Can you tell me how this happened?

SUBODH GUPTA: Over the last 20 years I shifted almost every two years from this studio to that studio, because all of them were rented places. Eventually, the landlord told us to go, and we had to go because people in the neighbourhood complained about the noise. So we faced many problems. We made all the works in little spaces for so many years. And, when some money came in, I thought it would be a dream to have our own studio. We have been building this for more than three years, four years almost.

HANS ULRICH OBRIST: You have obviously been very much involved in the process.

SUBODH GUPTA: Oh yes. With an architect friend who came and said, 'I'll do it for you.' So I said, 'Okay, let's do it.' We both sat down, I told him what the requirements were. I told him I need a hall, a big hall where I can work. In India, we don't have a studio concept. Many architects still haven't got a clue what a studio really is. For them, a space has no high ceiling. It is a functional place but not like a studio, the way artists need it. They need a really big space where they can make a sculpture, a painting. Where you can do big things and think about work very differently. So we had to intervene in the design part as well and we said, 'You can design the façade, but not the inside. Inside it will be block, block, block. Concrete and walls.'

HANS ULRICH OBRIST: Very often, artists have very specific light requirements for their studios. What was your light requirement?

SUBODH GUPTA: Light is very important in the studio and the designer did a good job with the lighting. I told him, 'Do what you like but I don't know how to bring light into a studio.' And he succeeded in doing that.

I don't know why, but we have too much dust in this country. The same amount of dust that you get in Europe in two months, we have in four hours. So we needed, for example, to cover the bookshelves with glass.

HANS ULRICH OBRIST: So it is natural light for the sculptures and for the paintings. In the last three, four decades, there has been a lot of discussion about this idea of a post-studio practice. But it seems to me, that for you the studio as a physical space has always played an important role.

SUBODH GUPTA: That depends on the artist. Some artists need a physical space. 'Physical' means making the work physically, whether it is a big work or a small work. So then the studio is very important. I don't know how Rirkrit Tiravanija works in the studio, since his work is very conceptual. Or how Richard Long works in the studio, since his work is outside. So it varies from artist to artist. Personally, I need a studio. I've always needed a studio.

HANS ULRICH OBRIST: How do you work exactly? Obviously you have assistants who help you with the painting. At the same time you are very involved yourself. How does the process start? Do you start with drawings, with sketches?

SUBODH GUPTA: I was trained as a painter. I've painted for 15 years. I know how to paint. I can still draw figures. I could draw your portrait right now. I do have an academic background in drawing, painting, and other classical disciplines. Now, of course, my practice has totally changed. I have assistants who paint for me. The ideas start basically in my iPhone. When I have an idea, I note it in my iPhone. That is like a drawing for me. The next day, when I come here, I think about this idea, I very rarely write things down, more often I do something practical.

HANS ULRICH OBRIST: Do you still draw?

SUBODH GUPTA: I do draw, but very little.

HANS ULRICH OBRIST: But you make sketches. Do you make drawings for the paintings as well?

SUBODH GUPTA: Only on the computer. Mostly I take photographs and work on the computer, with Photoshop and other things, and then draw it from there.

HANS ULRICH OBRIST: So it is more for the sculptures that you make sketches.

SUBODH GUPTA: Yes, sometimes – when necessary.

HANS ULRICH OBRIST: Do you also write?

SUBODH GUPTA: I do write sometimes. But I write in Hindi, because it is very comfortable for me. So I write in Hindi, then I speak to Flora [Boillot, the studio manager] and she puts it her way in her own words and then it goes to my other friends to refine it.

HANS ULRICH OBRIST: My studio visit with you started when I saw these found objects – stainless steel utensils. They are basically readymades, but you have occupied them so that they look like your works. We haven't spoken yet about this notion of appropriation. It doesn't seem with you to be 'appropriation-appropriation', it is more that you very often translate from a two-dimensional thing into a three-dimensional thing.

SUBODH GUPTA: For me, when I see the whole situation of the art world, it has become like a performance of just *being* there. For example, with very simple things:

Subodh Gupta, *C. B. II*, 2009

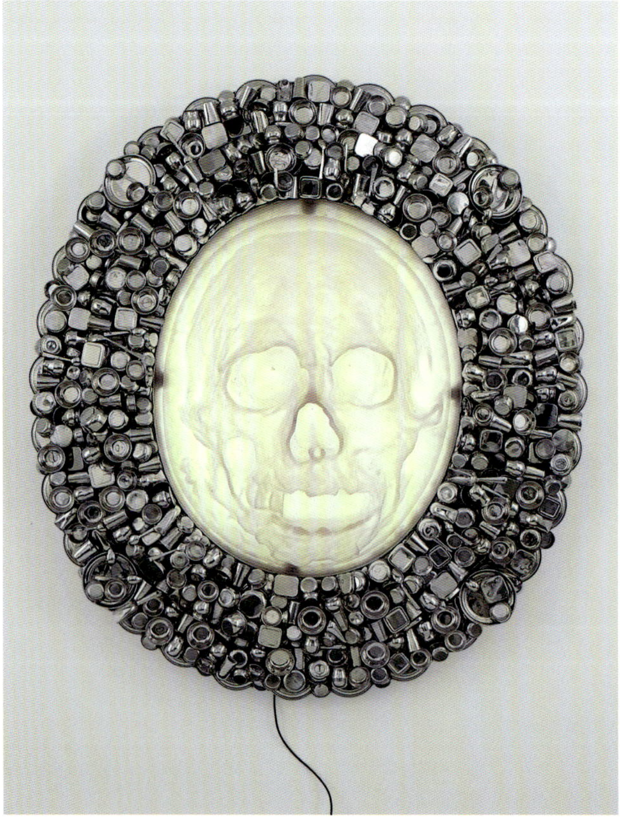

when I have clay in my hand, with water, and I try to create something. Or when I see somebody with flour and he begins kneading to make bread – in Hindi we call this 'gundna' – before the bread is ready to bake. For me, art is very much like this kneading process. With both hands you are working the dough to reach somewhere. So you keep doing it and keep doing it.

A notion of making art is also 'keep doing it, keep doing it, keep doing it', in the same way. Whether you make a sculpture, 3D, 2D. The beautiful part about art is not necessarily about if what you see is good or bad. Sometimes, just thinking about art and just standing still, at that moment, at that particular time, when you achieve something, it is as if a god has appeared before you! And that moment – nobody can feel your art except you. So I believe that we are the performers, it is a situation, where we are given a job to do.

HANS ULRICH OBRIST: That relates to your early performances. The performance never stopped. Is the idea of re-doing it connected to ritual? Repetition and difference?

SUBODH GUPTA: I did theatre, I did performance before, and that's why I never hesitate to use other media. I never know what will come next, what kind of practice. An artist has to go out of his/her comfort zone. That is the biggest fear for many artists and maybe I share that too.

HANS ULRICH OBRIST: So how to avoid that?

SUBODH GUPTA: Good question. I think there is a time when you feel like you have a ball and you are not going to get it in the goal. The ball will miss the net. It's a question of timing. It is great for an artist to be part of the atmosphere and to keep doing things. For me, *what is art* is not very important, *how to make art* is important. This idea of doing it.

HANS ULRICH OBRIST: How do inspirations occur in your work?

SUBODH GUPTA: I can tell you about a particular work, where my inspiration came from travelling. When I was at Tate Modern I saw the exhibition *Man Ray, Picabia and Duchamp*. While I was looking around I was very thrilled by their work and how the show was all put together – a very well curated show – I was very impressed. When I travel the world and I see people, see artists, and I hear people talking about artists, then afterwards I look them up and do some research. In the same way, when I saw Duchamp's drawing of the moustache on the *Mona Lisa* postcard, I was thrilled by this simple thing. And the idea came that I would make

Marcel Duchamp, *L.H.O.O.Q.*, 1919

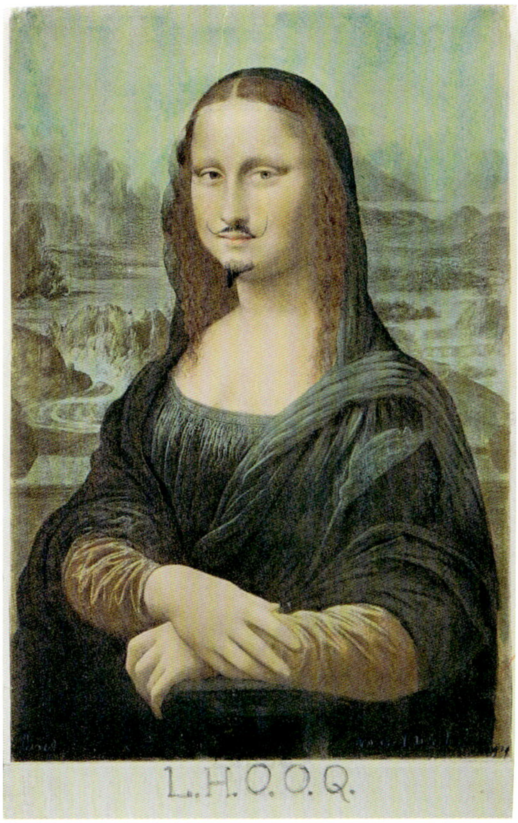

something out of this too. Duchamp is a distant figure, but his art is out there in the world, and many artists have reacted to his work, from his *Fountain* to many other works. I wanted to say something about him too. It is more like having a dialogue with Duchamp as an artist. I'll show you the piece I am making for the London show. I am making a sculpture of Duchamp's drawing on the *Mona Lisa* postcard. It is like having a dialogue with him. Just like saluting Duchamp.

HANS ULRICH OBRIST: I had a conversation the other day with Paul McCarthy where we discussed appropriation. He said, there are different forms of appropriation: for example, you can appropriate an object but, Paul said, for him appropriation is more a process than an object. He says, 'I am recycling objects or ideas', and I think in your case it is similar. Appropriation is not just a one-to-one transfer, it is a whole process.

SUBODH GUPTA: There is another piece where I reacted to the work of another artist, this time a work by Jeff Koons. But before I show you the photo, I must tell you how it started. I was in the south of France, visiting a collector's home, and suddenly, I saw a box lying there, with a Jeff Koons *Puppy*. It was really very fascinating for me, not only the piece of art by Jeff Koons, but perhaps even more so the box for this edition. I couldn't believe that the artist had made packaging like that for his own work of art. For me, that packaging became a work of art too. It is so fascinating, and I was not able to resist doing something. It took me time, because I had thought about this idea four years ago. But it took me time. Through friends I was finally able to ask Jeff Koons if I could do this work or not. Everybody told me, 'If you do it, he can sue you because you are not allowed to do it.' But I'd seen that he is a very nice man, such a nice man in fact that he would allow me to do it. My friend said to him, 'A friend of mine asked me if he could do it', and he said, 'Of course he can do it.'

HANS ULRICH OBRIST: So you basically re-did that box for the *Puppy*?

SUBODH GUPTA: I cast 50 of them in aluminium. His cardboard box looks like this. It is re-made in my material.

HANS ULRICH OBRIST: It is a very big edition.

SUBODH GUPTA: It is an unlimited edition, I think. I wanted to have a huge stack of them, like when you go to shops in Japan …

HANS ULRICH OBRIST: Jeff Koons inspires many younger artists. For example, Tino Sehgal has this Koons test. When a curator comes to see him, he says, 'Do you like Jeff Koons?' and if the curator says, 'No', he doesn't want to do the show … Can you tell me a bit more about what you like about Jeff Koons?

Prototype of *Jeff the Koons*
view at foundry

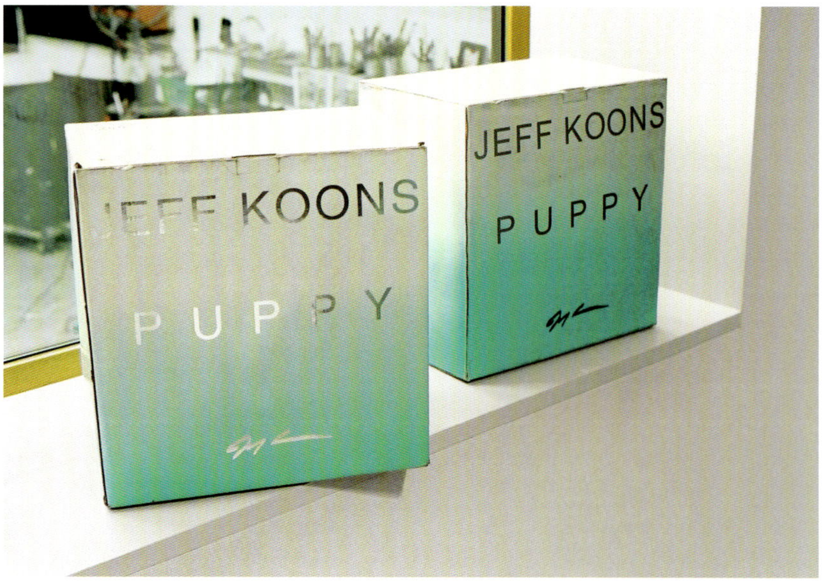

Jeff Koons, *Puppy (Vase)*, 1998
Edition of 3000

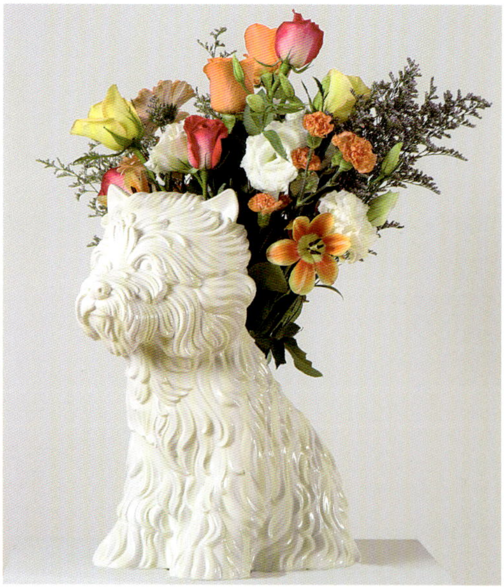

SUBODH GUPTA: I respect him a lot, because he has a tremendous amount of energy and he gives this energy to lots of artists from the younger generation all over the world: he gives us energy, he gives us fearlessness. Don't be afraid to do what you want to do. And that is the biggest achievement for any artist: not to be afraid of what you want to do. He really stands for that. I must say, that he created respect for the fearless artist. That's why I like him.

HANS ULRICH OBRIST: That is a beautiful definition, the idea of fearlessness. Your next big project is to exhibit in London, so it would be great to hear more about what will be in the show, besides the Duchamp and Jeff Koons homages.

SUBODH GUPTA: This is one section. In another section there will be *thalis*: stainless steel plates, but in a giant format, almost seven feet in diameter. I did the same piece before, but a small version. I put in oil and coins from all over the world. So I'm making that same piece eight feet in diameter.

HANS ULRICH OBRIST: In my interviews scientists often tell me about the moment when they made an invention. For instance, Benoît B. Mandelbrot told me about the special day when he invented the fractals. Your stainless steel series is, within your work so far, the most famous series, and I was wondering if you remember the day when you made this invention.

SUBODH GUPTA: It was in 1996, when I started changing my work. I was looking for what material to use, something that is very close to me. The kitchen is very important to me, since I love food and cook a lot myself. One day, while I was standing in the kitchen, I was looking at this rack, with stainless steel utensils – plates and cups. I kept looking at it and I was thinking, what am I going to do with this material. I looked at it ... and looked at it and suddenly, I saw it in front of me, and that was it. That was the very first piece. The first time I exhibited it was in 1999 in Bombay at Chemould Gallery. The piece was called *The Way Home I*. But I was playing with this material even before that.

HANS ULRICH OBRIST: Could we describe your work as minimalistic? Do you agree with that?

SUBODH GUPTA: I don't know, but why should I stop someone from viewing my work from his own perspective. In the same way, when you see, for example,

Subodh Gupta, *The Way Home I*, 1999
Installation view at Kwangju Biennale 2000

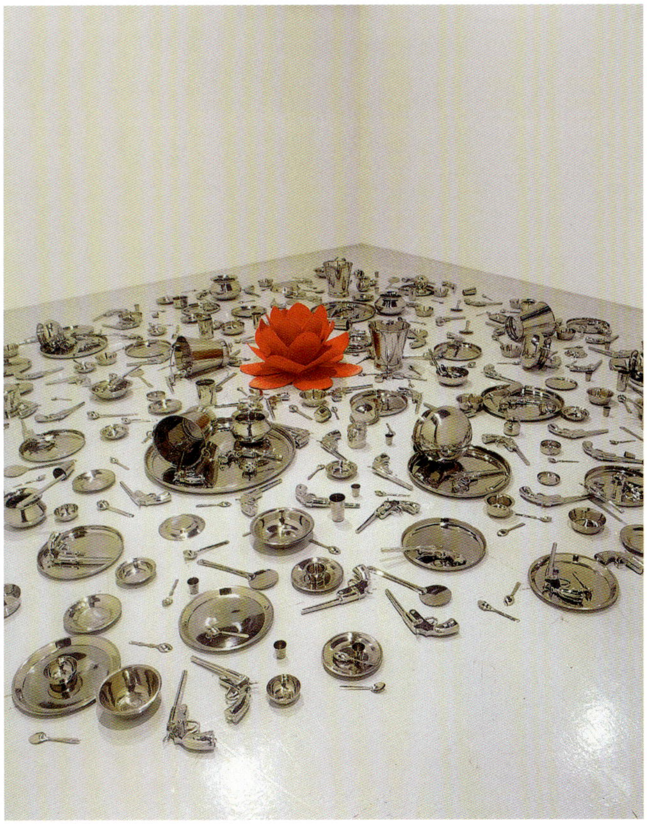

a cloud: the same cloud sometimes has a friendly face and other times a horrible face. In the same way as a cloud changes, there are things up here in your mind, and the way you see things is very special and very personal. It is an interpretation. I have no right to interfere there.

HANS ULRICH OBRIST: When we installed your stainless steel works for the first time, it was in Moscow, when Joseph Backstein, Daniel Birnbaum, Iara Boubnova, Nicolas Bourriaud, Rosa Martinez and I invited you to the first Moscow Biennale. The work appeared to me physically very much like something luxurious. But that is obviously a Western perspective. From an Indian perspective, it is almost the opposite. It is pretty banal.

SUBODH GUPTA: Similarly, when I used these objects for the first time, a friend of mine told me, 'Isn't it bizarre, you are using so many stainless steel utensils, and in India we have so many poor people who die every day from hunger and you are using them like this.' I totally agreed with him. In the same way, if you get up in the morning and you have a cup of tea or coffee, there is a cup and plate in front of you. But if there is no coffee or tea or food, it depicts hunger and hunger depicts death. In the same way food depicts life, so it is very easy to say life and death, but it is using a reality. The stainless steel utensils are such a common material in India. All of them, poor people, middle class families and rich people, use them. Every day, they use this old material to eat breakfast, lunch and dinner. So it is very much related…

I'm making three plates like this and each plate will be a different work. One with coins, one with – I cannot explain – and this is the thing that I am going to put on the third plate: old shoes used by labourers and workers. It is like worshipping them. When I see that symbol, it is not just a footprint, it also shows the way the person used it. And the way they leave their mark, their footprint on their own sandals, from day to day, wearing them every day, and at the same time showing how much this person worked. It is about hard labour. And these people are very close to god, I believe. They are not thinking about you and me, they are just thinking about their life and their bread and butter, how they can survive. It is a trace of survival. And they are the people I want to worship. So the *thalis* will be the main pieces in the show.

HANS ULRICH OBRIST: You have used a figurative language in some works, but then something happens at a certain moment and it turns abstract. These black pieces that I saw in the studio last time, when you used these painted stainless steel pincers in 2007/2008, you kind of leave the representational ground, they become more abstract.

Subodh Gupta, *Untitled*, 2008

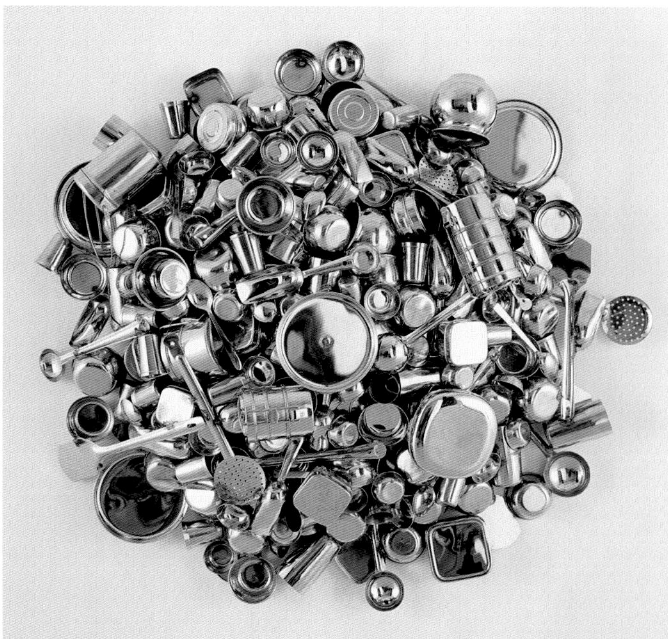

SUBODH GUPTA: Artists do not always think about it very deeply when they do something, while they are trying to make something. Sometimes you pick up a pencil and not necessarily try to make a portrait but the pencil moves. In the same way for me, when I start making a sculpture, I might try to do one thing and it becomes something very different. I like that. And maybe even I don't understand what it means and why I am doing it. But I love doing it because I myself created a form, which I do not even necessarily understand. Honestly, when I am making it, I might not understand what I am doing. It is the practice of the moment, where I go somewhere else, where you maybe don't even try to go. I like that whole feeling and that idea, it is almost like the climax of masturbating.

HANS ULRICH OBRIST: What happens here is that you use these stainless steel pincers and they are obviously not cups, they are not objects, they are kind of abstract elements. What led to that? Why these pincers?

SUBODH GUPTA: In school we were given short stories to read by the Indian writer Munchi Premchand, from the early 19th century. He is one of the best writers in this country. He wrote a story with the title *Hamid Ka Chimta*. Hamid is the name of the boy, and Chimta means the tong: the tong of Hamid. It is about how his grandmother gives him a penny and says, go to this fair and have a good time. So the boy can choose between a slice of cake or a cup of ice cream. He has just enough money to choose one thing and he buys a tong and takes it home. The grandmother says, 'Why did you buy this tong?' And he explains, because when she makes bread, she always burns her fingers, and the boy thought about his grandmother's fingers that were always getting burned. It is a sentimental story, but it is also relevant to the day-to-day life, to the reality of a middle-class family.

HANS ULRICH OBRIST: Let's talk about colours. Here you have red, so it is no longer the stainless steel. Carlos Cruz-Diez, this pioneer of Kinetic art, says that colour is dynamic, it is an evolving event. What is colour for you?

SUBODH GUPTA: No doubt muted and vibrant colours are always two kinds of colours for me. Muted means grey colours. I have an affinity to them but as soon as I move away from grey, I go for very bright yellow and red, immediately. I don't mix in between. For a long time, I did a lot of painting in blue colours. So the notion of colour depends very much on the mood. I don't know what happens psychologically.

HANS ULRICH OBRIST: So you had a blue period, like Picasso …

SUBODH GUPTA: I wouldn't go that far, but yes, I painted many paintings in blue.

HANS ULRICH OBRIST: Then there is a brown period …

Subodh Gupta, *Black Thing,* 2007

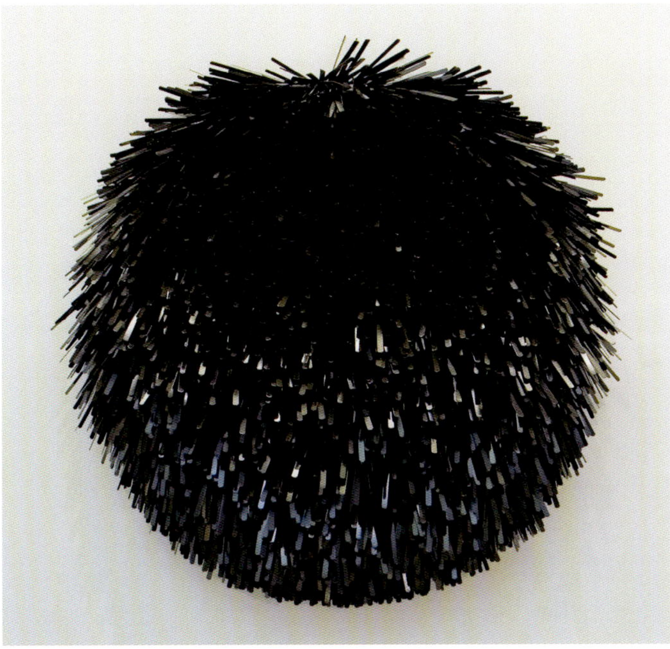

SUBODH GUPTA: This is a natural colour, it is cow dung, so it is brown in itself.

HANS ULRICH OBRIST: So you don't have a favourite colour. It changes.

SUBODH GUPTA: I don't have a favourite colour. But if you ask me, to be honest, I like mute colours more.

HANS ULRICH OBRIST: What about the other pieces in the London show?

SUBODH GUPTA: There is another piece that you will see in the show: a gigantic spoon. I put two spoons together. It is a gigantic double spoon. It is like spooning, the way lovers do sometimes.

And I made this other piece, but I am not sure if it will be in the show.

HANS ULRICH OBRIST: *Art will kill you.* Can you tell me about this?

SUBODH GUPTA: I did this piece about two years ago, when art was at its climax in terms of the market and the way things had gone so berserk. People hardly respected each other anymore and everybody started to think, 'I am so big'.

HANS ULRICH OBRIST: When there was this whole hype.

SUBODH GUPTA: Even travelling, and the way people started to talk. It became too much about hitting direct. It was not a very good time for an artist, apart from the money aspect.

With the background of that fear and that pressure, I made *Art will kill you*. Now is a good moment. It is much more relaxed. It is again about art, it is again a peaceful time for people who respect art.

I cast these potatoes. They are the exact size of real potatoes and they look like potatoes. I did not paint them. It is just a cast bronze potato. It looks exactly the same. I kept it like that.

Another piece: I made a tree. A tree that I saw in my hometown. The tree grew through a window, inside a house, and grew out of it on the other side. I was very fascinated with the root in the wall and I cast this tree. It will be in the show too.

HANS ULRICH OBRIST: So it is a tree that grows together with a house. Almost like a hybrid between a human construction and a construction of nature.

SUBODH GUPTA: What I've added to the tree is a wall and the wall is broken. Sometimes nature makes its own art. I sometimes get very inspired by looking at nature and seeing such things.

HANS ULRICH OBRIST: What is the role of titles in your work?

SUBODH GUPTA: It is similar to that of the work of Duchamp, I suppose. The title of the tree might be *Suppression*.

HANS ULRICH OBRIST: You always give titles to the pieces. *Giant Leap of Faith*; *All Things are Inside*; *Everything is Inside*. How do you find your titles?

SUBODH GUPTA: First of all, I always think about the reason behind making the piece and that is where the title comes from. In that sense, the title of the Jeff Koons piece will be *Jeff the Koons*.

Subodh Gupta, *Art will kill you*, 2008

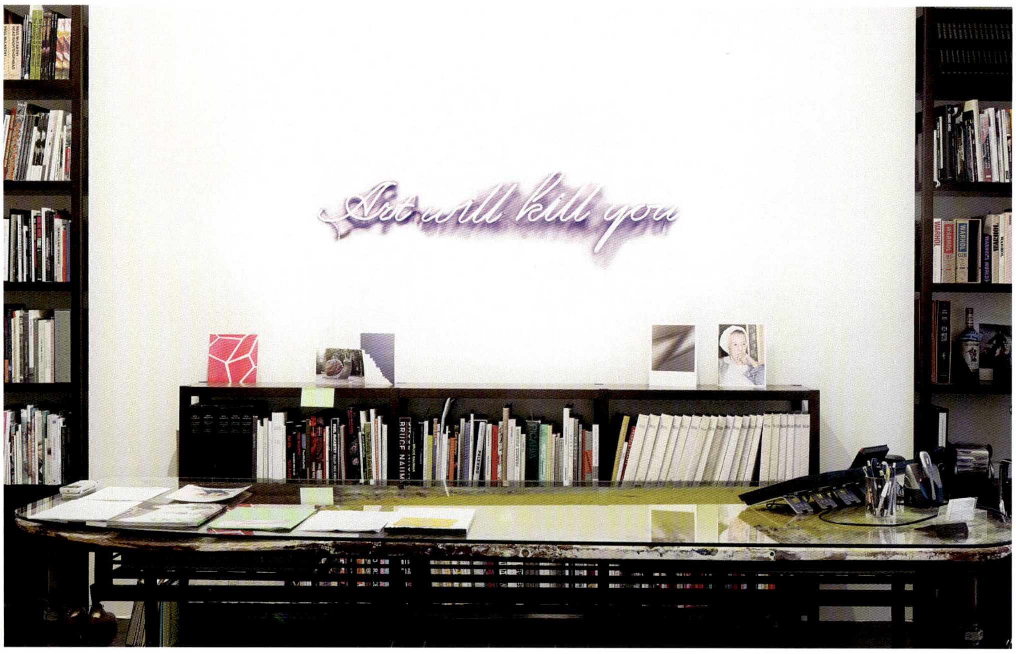

HANS ULRICH OBRIST: Have the Internet and the computer changed the way you work?

SUBODH GUPTA: Of course. In the past, the pencil was the computer for the artist. Today, the computer has become the pencil for us.

HANS ULRICH OBRIST: Yet, in this computer age, we still do a lot of physical stuff, for example books. We're doing this interview not for the Internet, but for a physical book. I was wondering, what is the role of books for you? Are you involved in your books, or do you let other people do them?

SUBODH GUPTA: I'm closely involved with the process. In 2008 we did my book *Gandhi's Three Monkeys*. Flora Boillot, my studio manager, played a big part in it, and Akshay Raj Singh Rathore designed the book together with me. We did it together, in-house. It is a very personal book.

HANS ULRICH OBRIST: Any other books?

SUBODH GUPTA: No, but I love to do books. That is why I say artists should spend more time in their studio on their own, so that they can do more things.

Patna City, Bihar

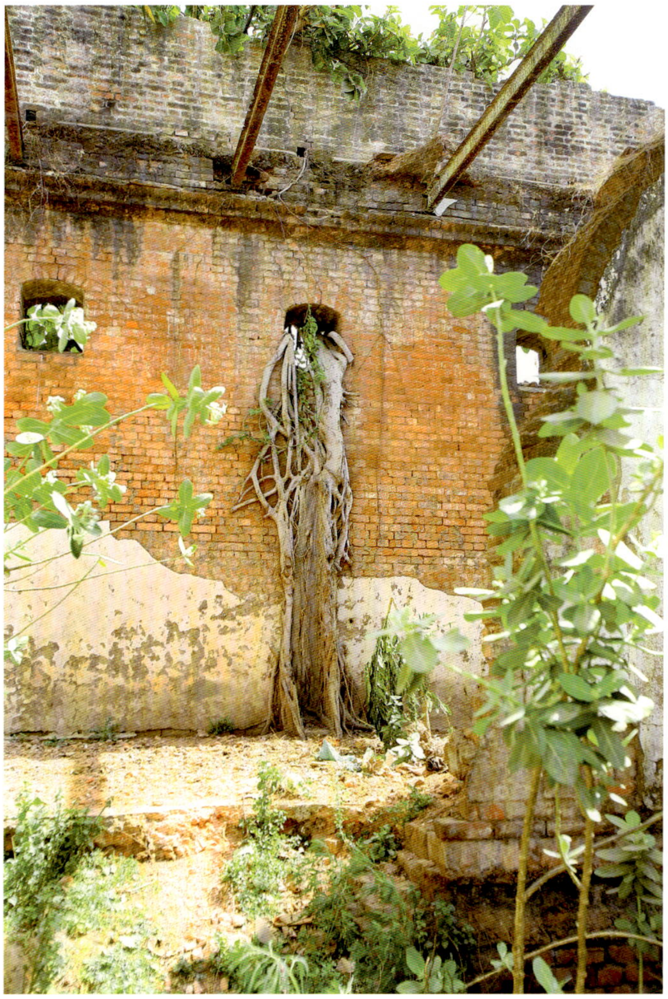

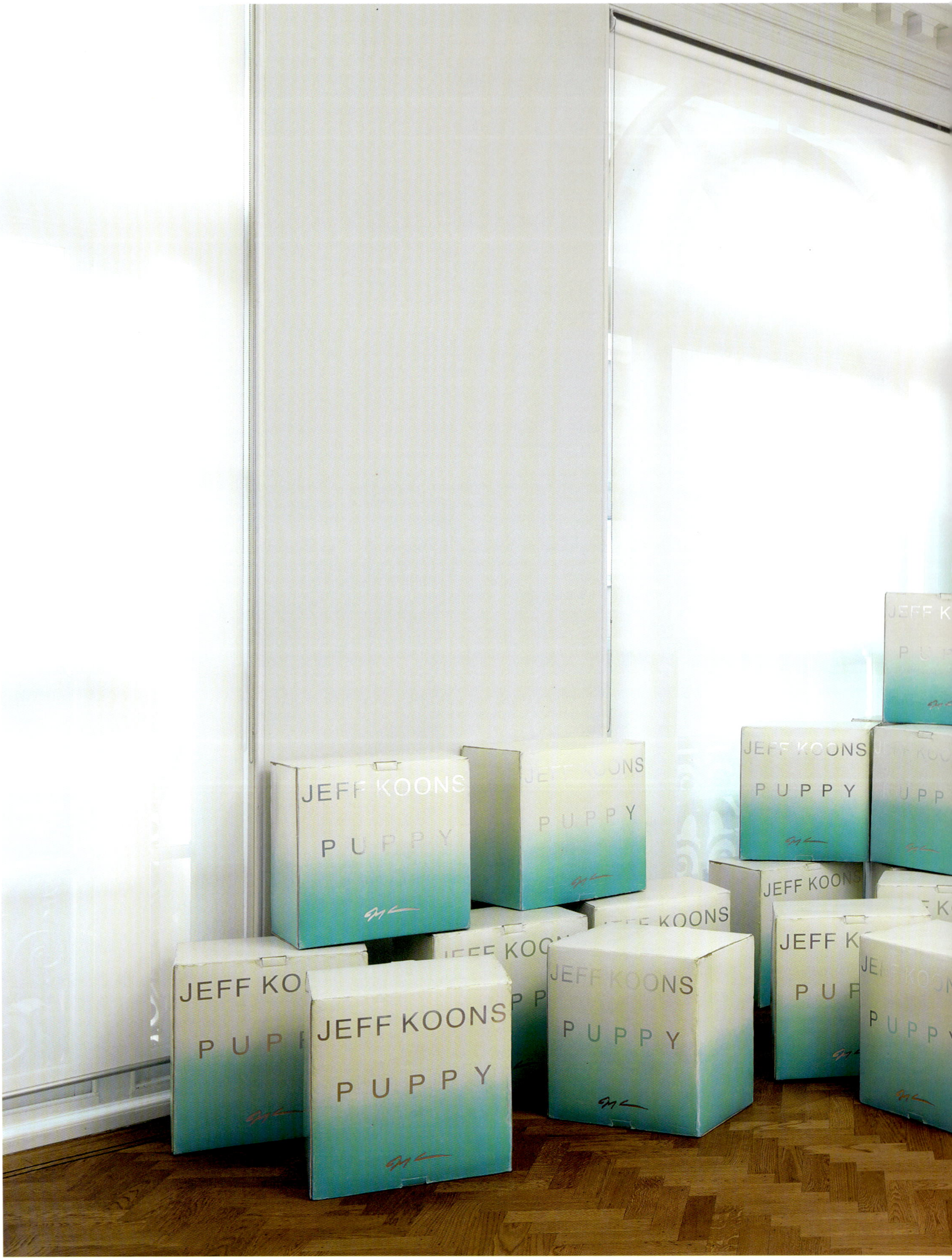
JEFF KOONS
PUPPY

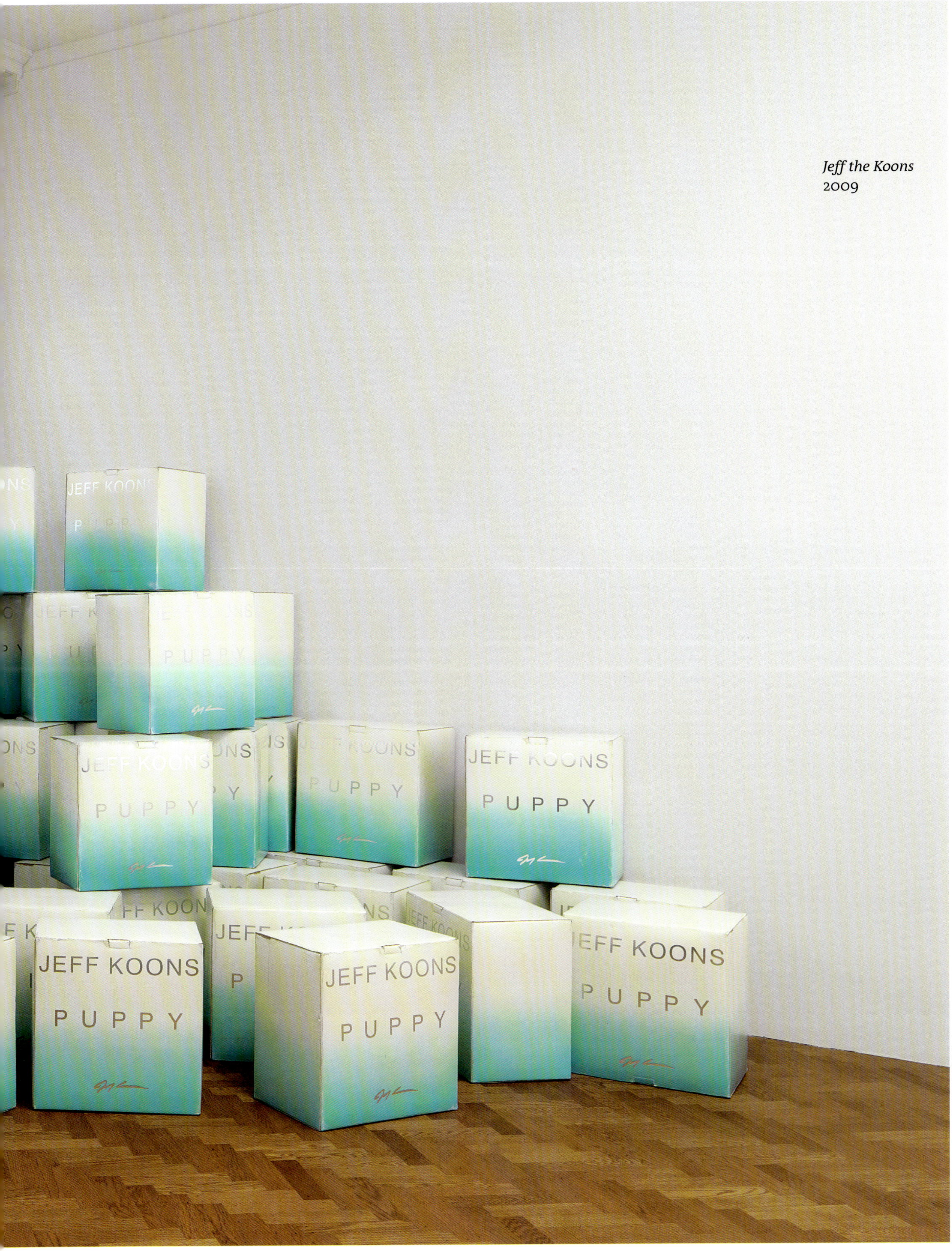

Jeff the Koons
2009

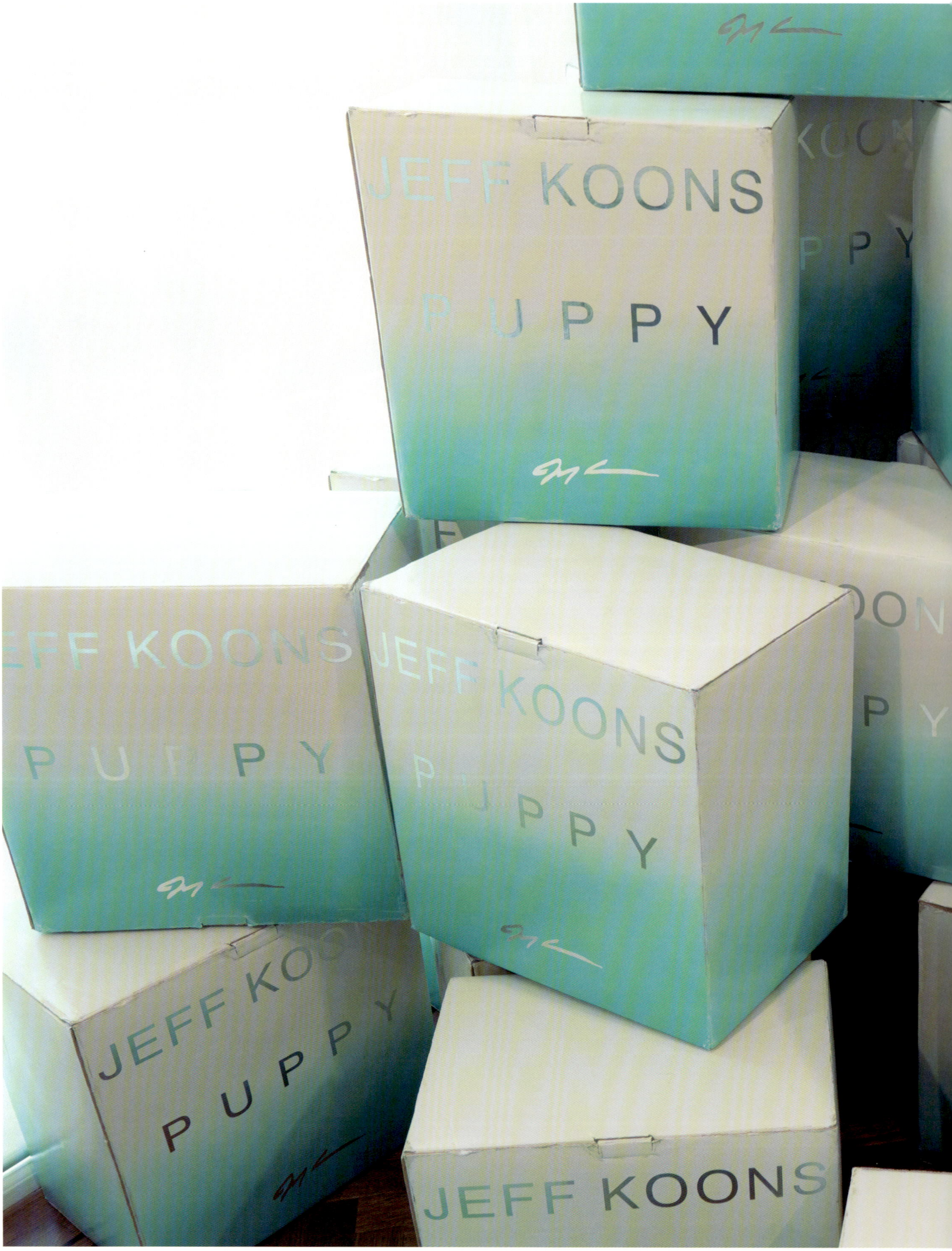
JEFF KOONS
PUPPY
JEFF KOONS
PUPPY
JEFF KOONS
PUPPY
JEFF KOONS
PUPPY
JEFF KOONS

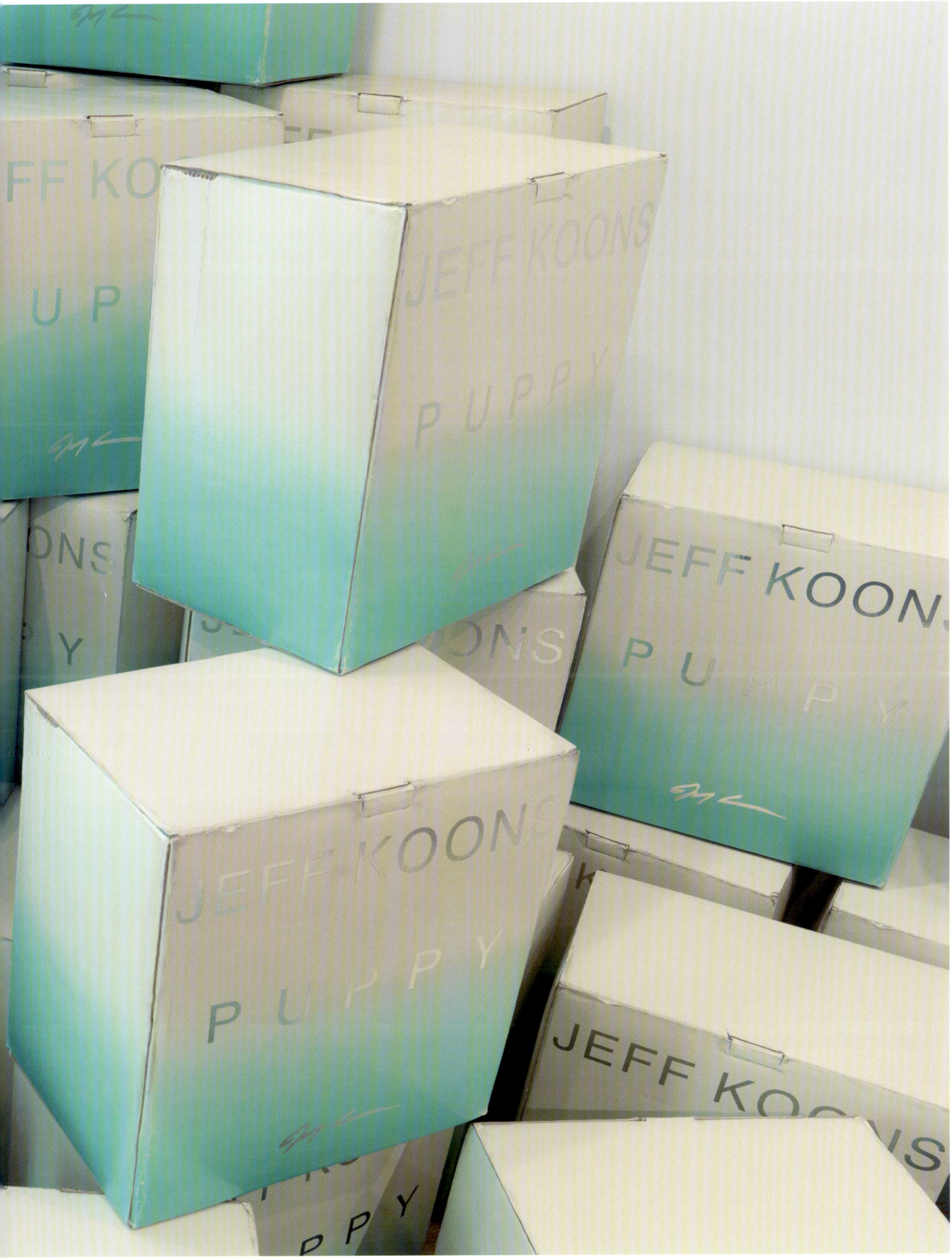
JEFF KOONS
PUPPY

Et tu, Duchamp?
2009

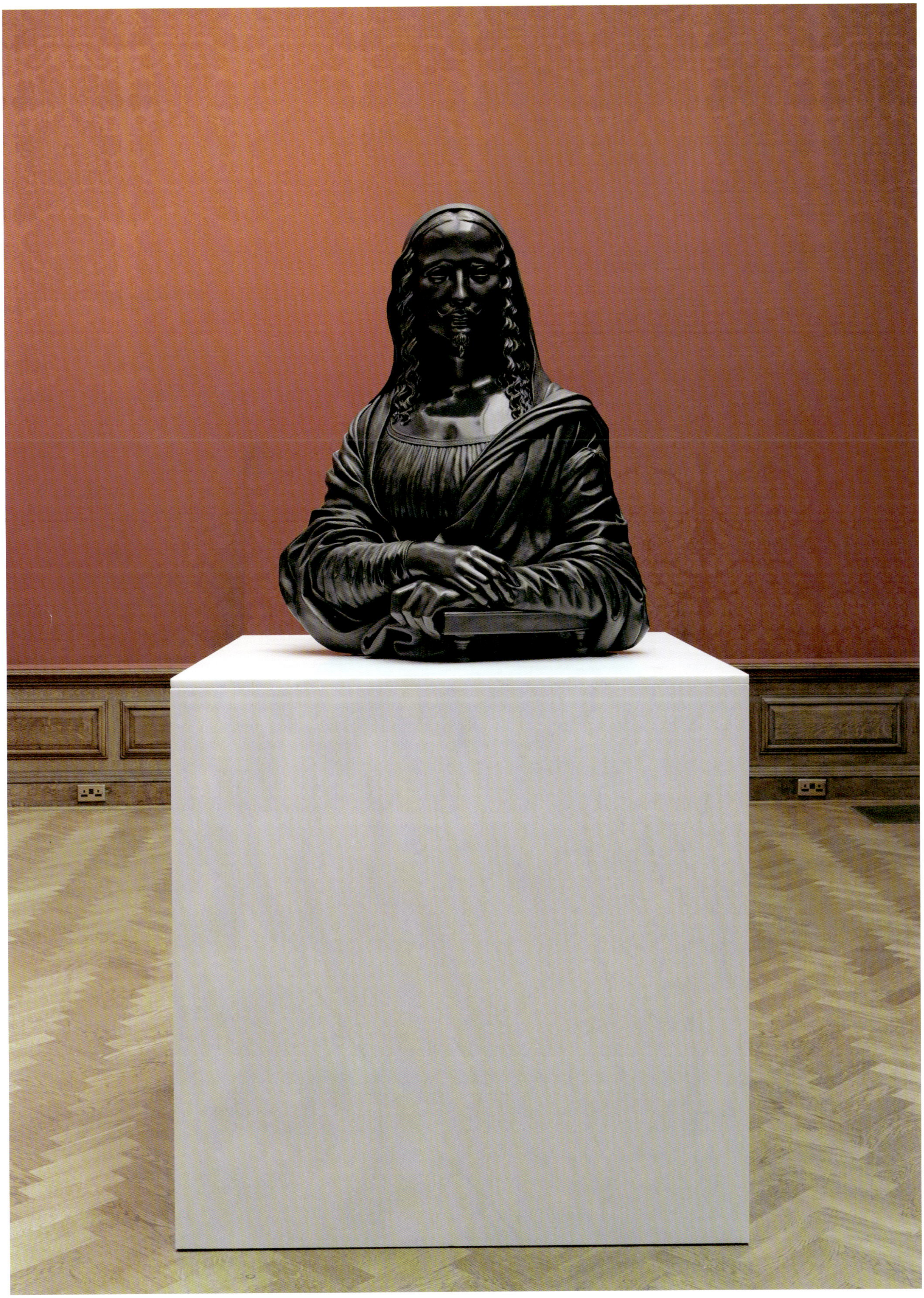

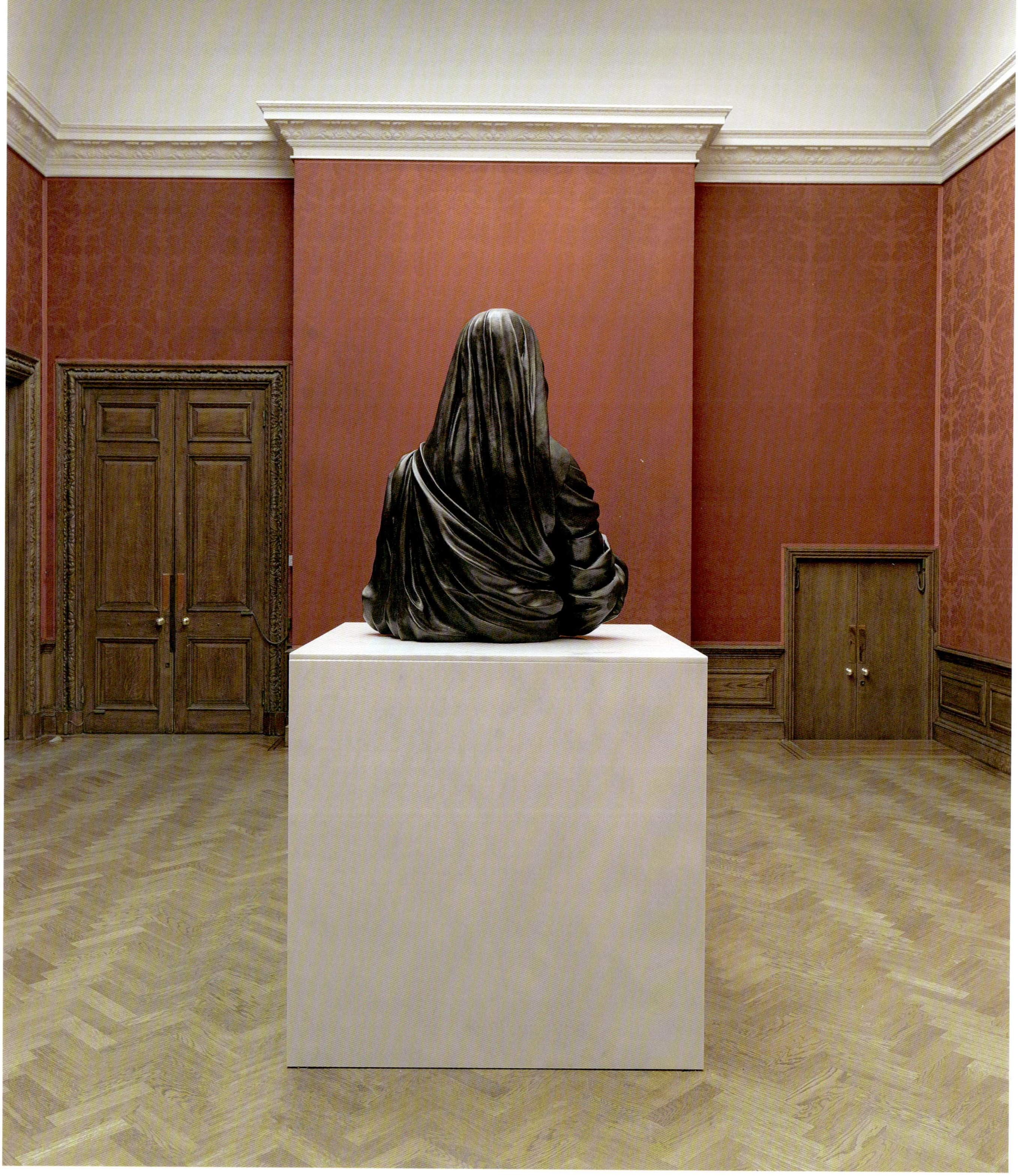

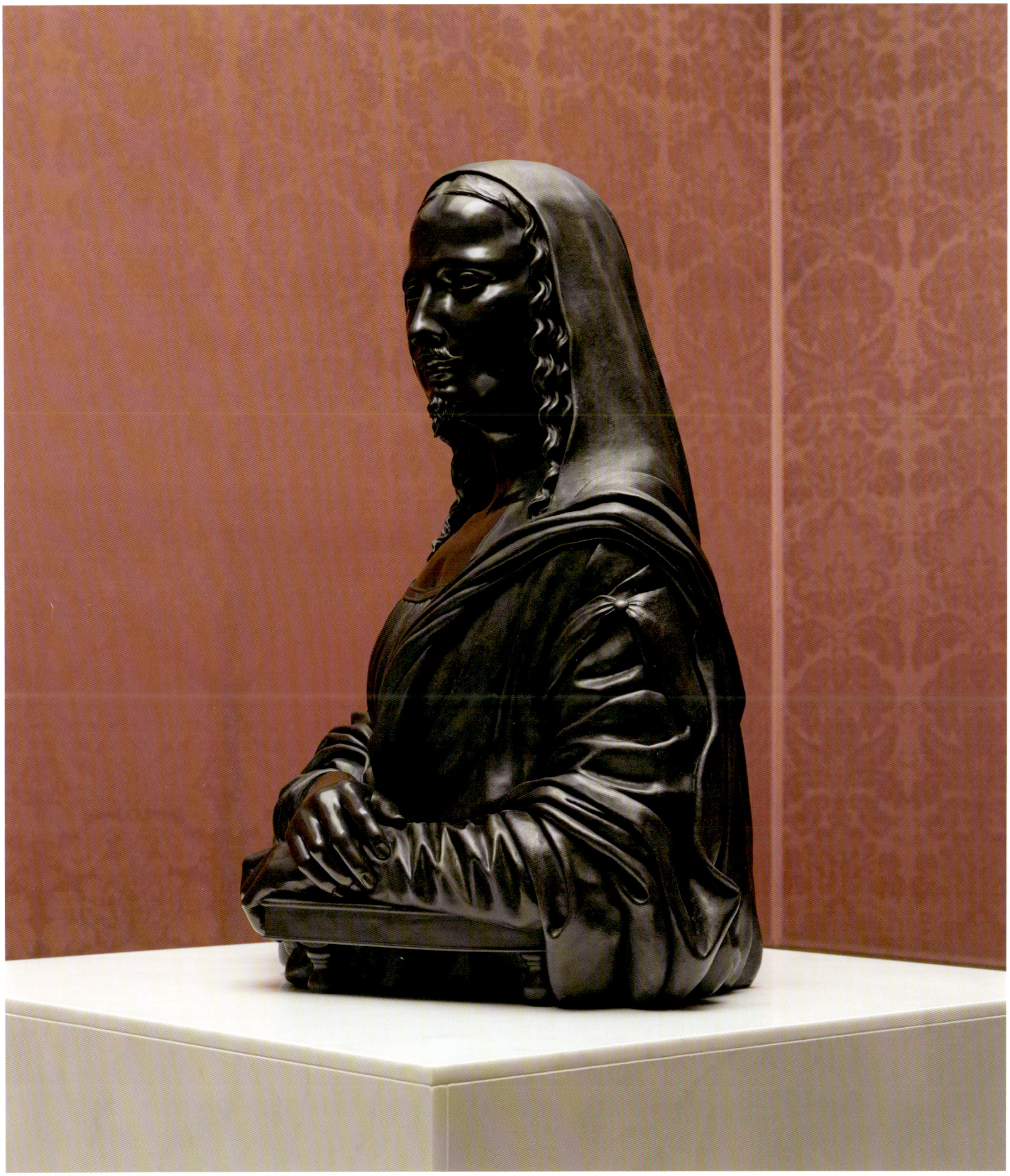

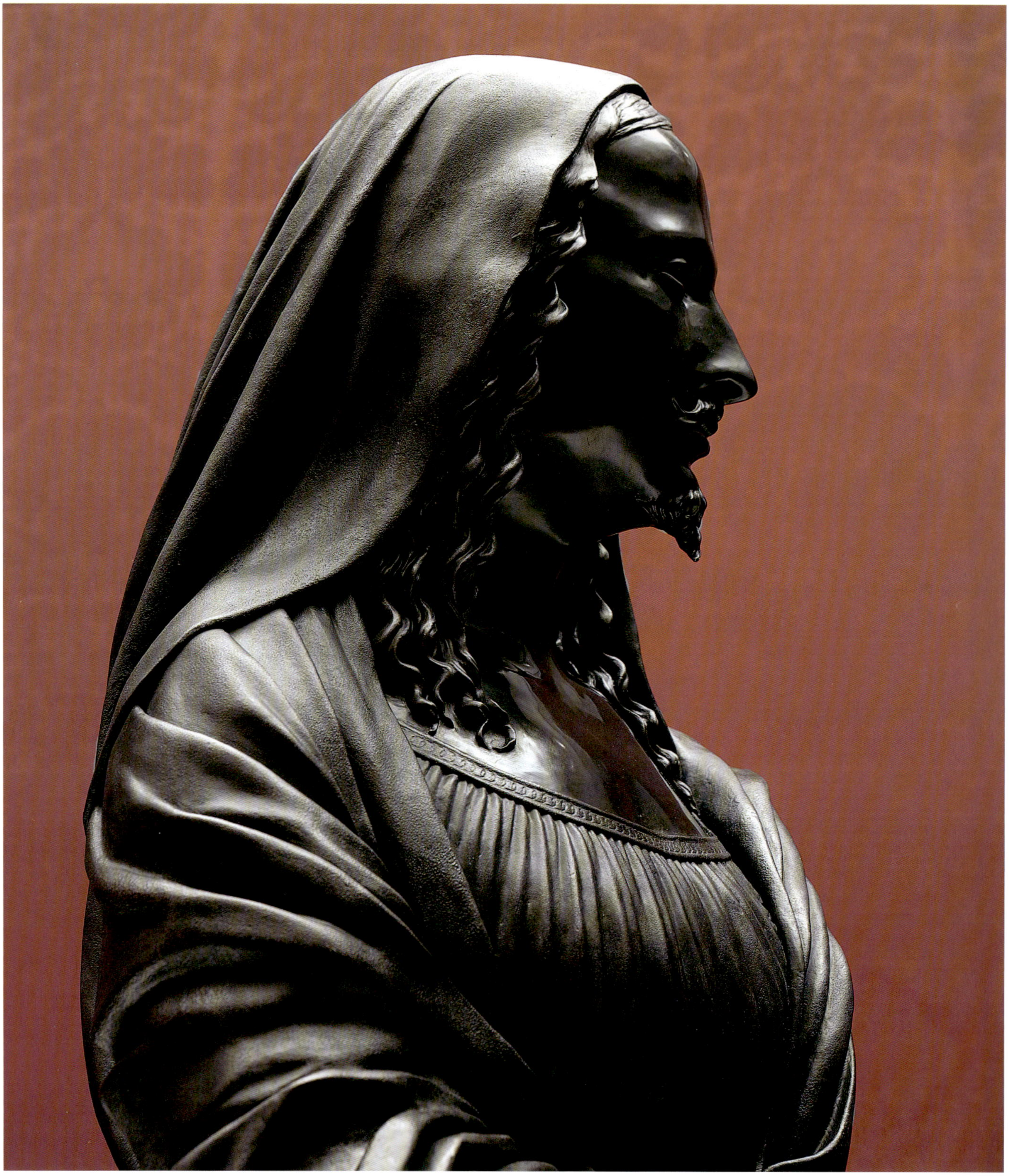

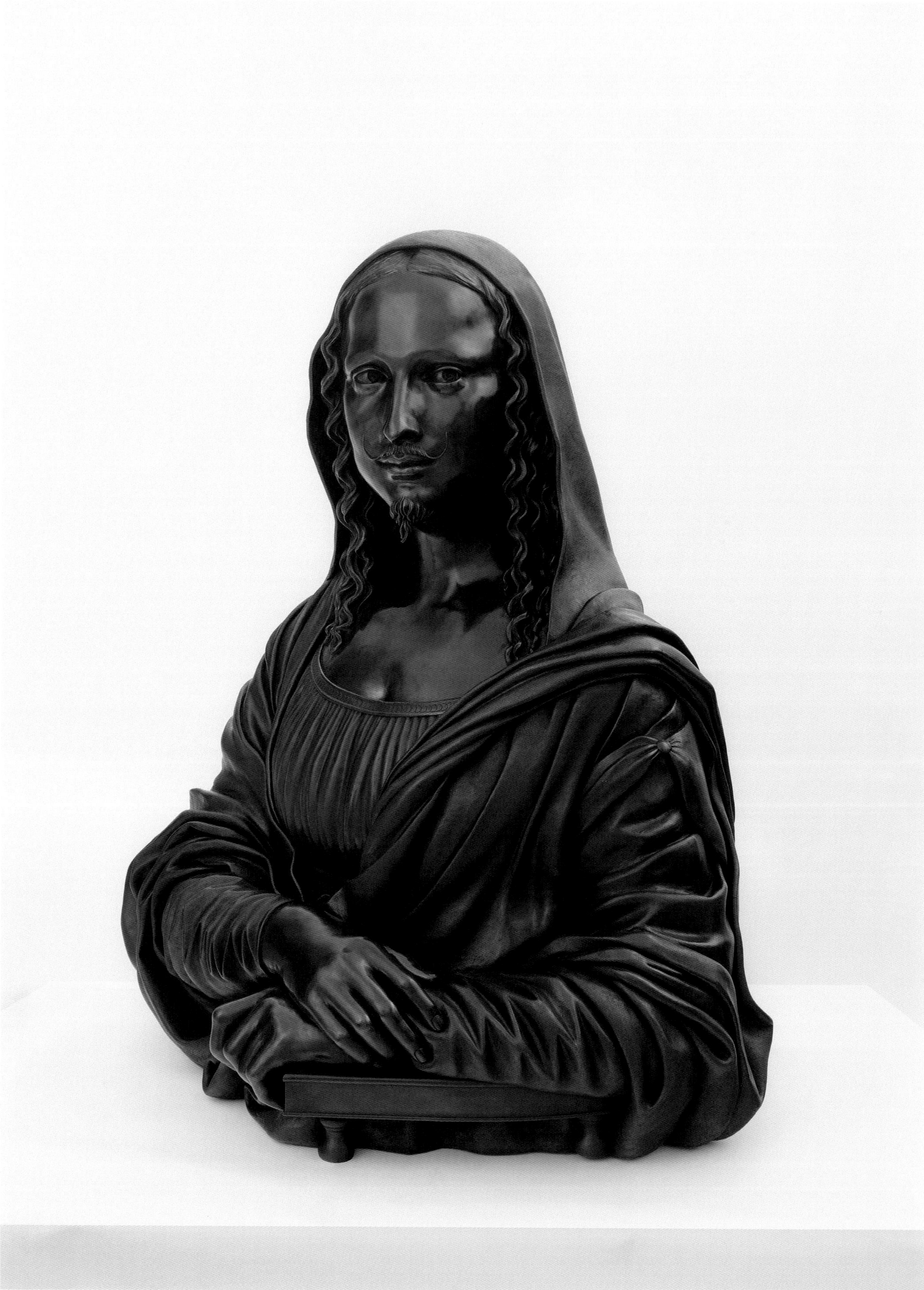

Speak, See, Remember: On Subodh Gupta

by Martin Herbert

One autumn day in 1919, Marcel Duchamp bought an inexpensive postcard reproduction of the *Mona Lisa* on Paris's rue de Rivoli, took it home, pencilled a moustache on La Gioconda's face and subtitled the defaced image with the letters *L.H.O.O.Q.*, which, as every art student knows, sounds like 'elle a chaud au cul' (she has a hot ass) when read aloud. 'Its repercussions have not yet died down', wrote Calvin Tomkins in 1996 of the Frenchman's traducing of tradition via his deadliest 'assisted readymade'. Not entirely, anyway. If Duchamp can be said to have created the *lingua franca* of contemporary art, it is a language that among Western practitioners might easily be taken for granted. In other news, I saw *L.H.O.O.Q.* in a gallery a few months ago. Ninety years old, it looked – unsurprisingly – historical. It was difficult to see, in fact, its detonative charge weakened by diffusion across countless artworks since its making (and by later, weaker mockeries of the *Mona Lisa*), those selfsame artworks increasingly reinforcing suspicions that vivifying the familiar object via art is a pursuit of steadily diminishing returns.

Subodh Gupta's *Et tu, Duchamp?* (2009) isn't precisely a readymade, though it is something close to an assisted readymade of an assisted readymade, the original appropriating impulse squared. More definitely, this three-dimensional, larger-than-real-life rendering in black bronze of Duchamp's defiling of Leonardo is a palimpsest of intents, one which permits a multifariously weird experience: that of sneaking up from behind on an enlarged, three-dimensional, negative version of an already-androgynous remake of Western civilisation's most famous two-dimensional image. Moreover, it is an act of possession, superficially of an icon but more deeply of a language: one which, within art, remains *the* dominant language: the conceptual and, to some extent, anti-retinal. Today, making such a claim – an assertion of the right to speak – means nothing if the artist is from New York; it's a cultural inheritance, for better or worse, a virtual birthright, gift-as-impediment. It means something, however, if they are from (or at least working in) New Delhi. In Gupta's hands, the appropriated and re-presented object has itself a kind of material to be reshaped. It was always, on one level, a method of making things visible. Here, that permission is seized upon, and assumes new dimensions which scale down to the local and up to the global.

When a language travels – laboriously, in India's pre-Internet 1990s, via contemporary art periodicals that Gupta would sedulously request from London-based friends – the syntax and vocabulary changes; the accent shifts. These are axioms of descriptive linguistics. Simultaneously impish and serious, Gupta pushes and leverages such slippages, plays with their rich concomitant ironies, felicities of mistranslation. The result is that he, wryly starting from a Duchampian position, can put low, commonplace, culturally specific objects into a Western gallery – the ubiquitous, stainless-steel tiffin boxes, lunch pails, pans and utensils that India's 1.2 billion people use automatically every day – and have them appear, when accreted in large numbers, as both visually dazzling and trailing implications about a subcontinent's latter-day economic rise. Such works elevate a local commodity as deftly as the vitrined vacuum cleaners of Jeff Koons' *The New* (1980–1987), and it is wholly comprehensible that Gupta nods to Koons (and, along the way, Warhol, the connective tissue between Koons and Duchamp) via *Jeff the Koons* (2009), his recent array of fifty *trompe l'oeil* versions in painted aluminium of the box which contained the American artist's 1998 porcelain multiple, *Puppy (Vase)*. It is the formal language of the original, giant West Highland terrier – made from live flowers – which Gupta recasts in his aggregates of steel.

Et tu, Duchamp?
2009

Simultaneously, however, he bends the function of the readymade, making it almost talismanic, generously so, reversing its parameters. When Gupta, in *Aam Aadmi* (2009), presents a boxful of intricately faked, painted bronze mangoes in hay, or, in *I believe you* (2009) a seven foot stainless steel *thali* half-filled with worn-down sandals, trainers, moccasins and flip-flops, he is speaking affirmatively of a formative culture's trappings. (He is also playing a clever, destabilising game of perception, mixing together in a single exhibition real 'found' objects and intricate fakes.) So, too, in a feat of casually cosmopolite relativism, is Gupta talking about subjective influence when he echoes Duchamp or Koons. This, furthermore, is a rhetorical move that has the additional upshot of making one see their achievements afresh, refracted through Gupta's culturally specific manoeuvring in the narrow airspace that remains after them. (For all its strategising, his art doesn't have to exclude the courteous acknowledgement of presiding influence, an approach increasingly rare amid the Oedipal gyrations of art from the modern era onwards.) And in each case the artwork is a kind of staging. It partakes of theatre, of eye-catching effects. (There is showmanship, even, in taking the worldly object somewhere new, with such ostentatious fleetness.)

In Gupta's case, theatre is stratagem. The art world is an economy of attention, and there are plenty of artists in it who, for better or worse, use spectacle simply in order to gain that attention. Gupta, it is worth pointing out, worked with a small theatre troupe for four or five years in his native region of Khagaul, in Bihar. It is perhaps worth defining as effects his use of optical dazzle, gargantuan scale, technical counterfeiting and the pointed, head-turning, culturally specific gesture (e.g. *Black and White*, 2009, a pair of rotating, swastika-shaped ceiling fans which remind us that the design, its name coming from the Sanskrit *svástika*, was first a Hindu religious symbol). They command attention, in the first place, from which point Gupta can not only assert himself and his entitlement to speech in the Esperanto of art, but also proceed on a programme of deliberate, good-humoured one-upping with regard to art history. Consider *Master Bet* (2009), twenty-nine blue watercolour body prints which trump Yves Klein's 1958 development of 'living brushes' by using, assumedly, the artist's own genitals; or reconsider *Et tu, Duchamp?*, such a flamboyant amplification of the earlier artist's concept, or Gupta's other appropriations of appropriations. It is notable in these recent examples that the artist doesn't feel the consistent necessity to insert overtly 'Indian' signifiers into his art; one may consider that shearing away a rhetorical move in itself. If his earlier work used invention, wit and unexpected switchback moves to ventriloquise the tautological idea of its own right to representation within the global art world, some of his newer proposals might seemingly assert that Gupta no longer needs to leverage his ethnicity in any way, for all that this is not the same as relinquishing it.

Now, in a sentence like that, one may be tempted to substitute 'an Indian artist' for Gupta's name. This is the central snare of interpreting his work: the risk of using him as shorthand for his changing homeland, as many commentators have done. Gupta's art, they say, has narrated his country's accelerated rise as an economic power (and indeed, a number of works in recent years have seemed specifically to address issues of Indian militarism). His masses of utensils, the voices continue, narrate the tenets of a new, increasingly technological India, the world's most heavily populated democracy, where sheer numbers matter and where old signifiers no longer apply; and his outdoing of the cultural canon has similar parallels in India's own growing confidence. These readings, I would argue, are corollaries of Gupta's effects. His art can stand being mobilised as social commentary: he is surely aware of that and has benefited from it in terms of his own visibility. But where it remains most profoundly culturally specific, I'd argue – and unsurprisingly, given the artist's facility for misdirection – is in another aspect.

Aam Aadmi
2009

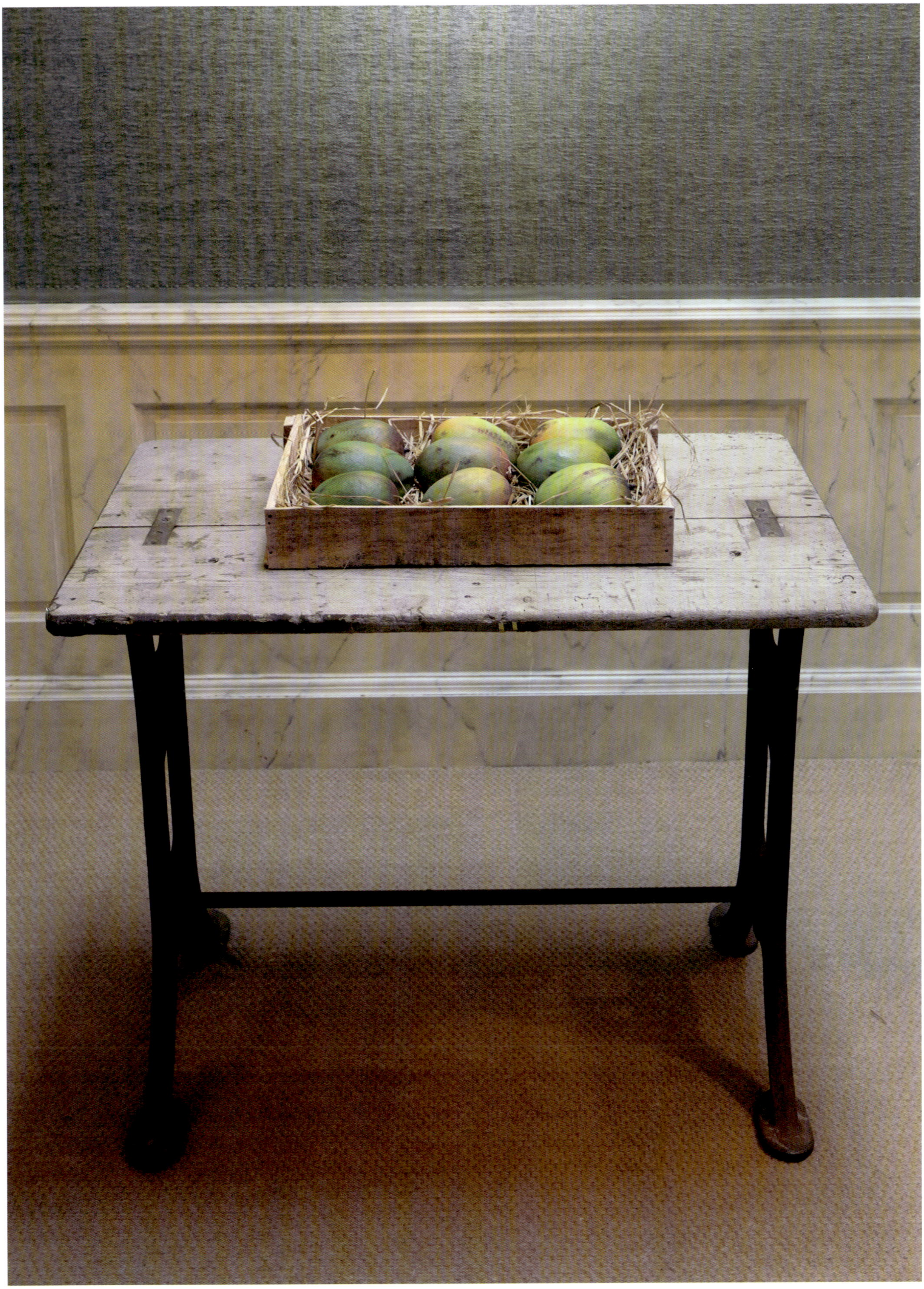

Not long ago, Gupta found a tree bursting out of a wall in his hometown: a kind of crazy waterfall in wood. It later appeared to emerge from a brick-framed aperture in Hauser & Wirth's London gallery, descending anarchically towards a half-shattered brick wall. This was, on first glance, an utter interpenetration of two cultures, an irruption of a natural and earthy hemisphere into the refined Lutyens architecture of the gallery. Except, of course, that what looked like a readymade really wasn't: Gupta had cast the original tree in fibreglass and had it meticulously painted, and it emerged from a fake wall. The mind behind *Wall* (2009) was evidently aware of and toying with multiple expectations; and his production might be said to be more sophisticated than the world it entered. In that respect, this was a typically layered, assured and droll example of Gupta's showmanship and ability to engender the purposeful double take.

But it was something else, too, which hid in plain sight: a literal modelling and exposure of roots. Whatever rhetorical heights Gupta's art might reach – and, again, it has proved uncommonly adaptable to weighty socio-political narratives – it emerges from dimensions of respect for the local but decisive: for types of tradition, for the soil out of which its maker has grown and continues to grow. How India's own advances intersect with its deep entrenchment in millennia-old custom is, perhaps, a more probing question raised by Gupta's work than simply how the latter narrates a subcontinent's rise. But what can feel most salient and durable about his art are the implicit ramifications of its absorbing, reflecting and reconciling of cultural diversities. This made me, Gupta's art says, pointing in turn to exhausted footwear and shining steel buckets and a continuum of advanced engagements with the re-presented object, making them visible. This made me. It's mine, it's ours. I'm speaking the language, in my voice. Listen.

And we do, and it starts from there.

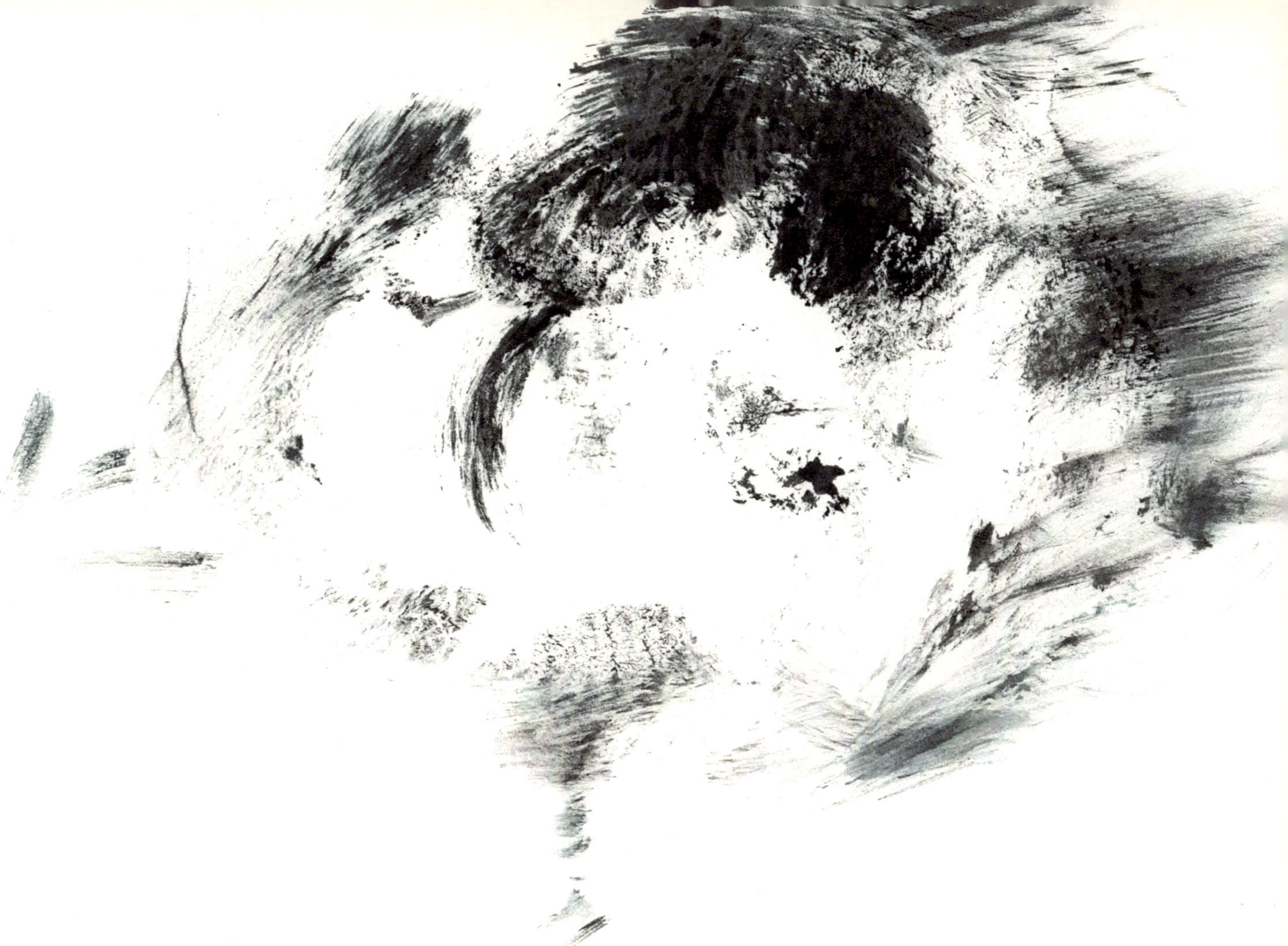

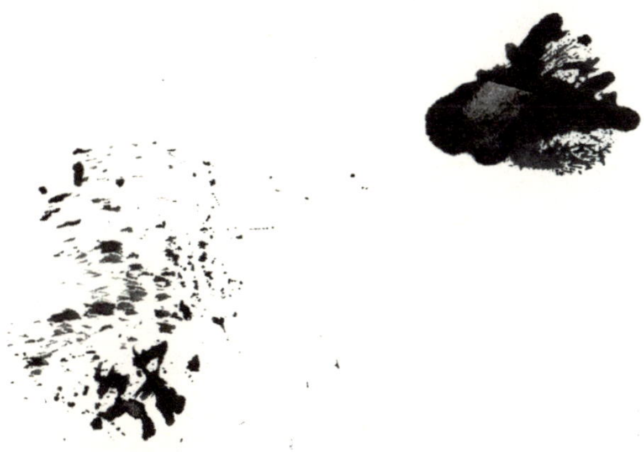

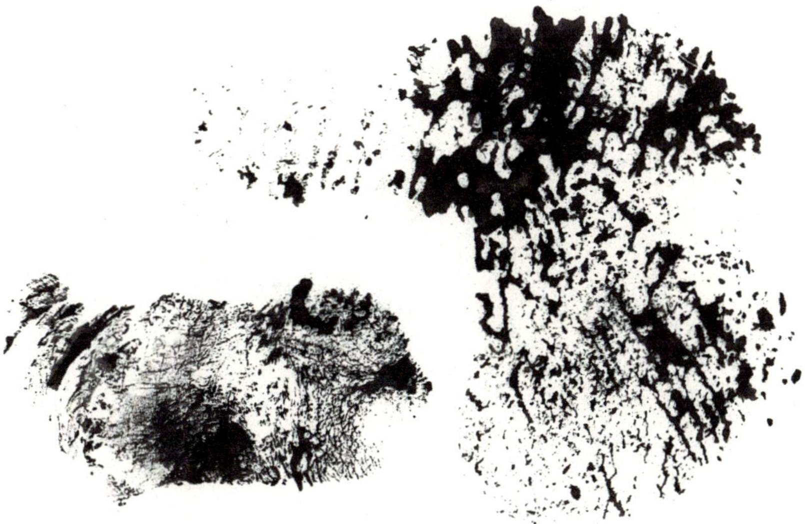

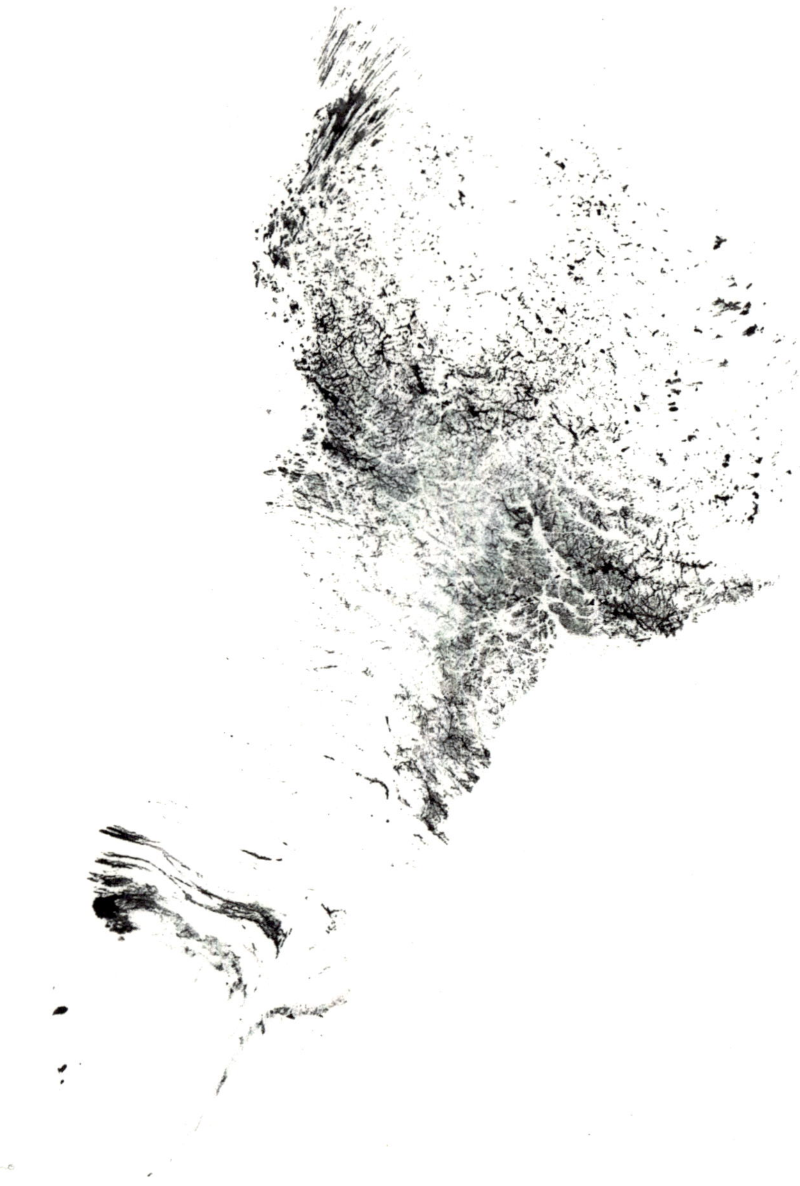

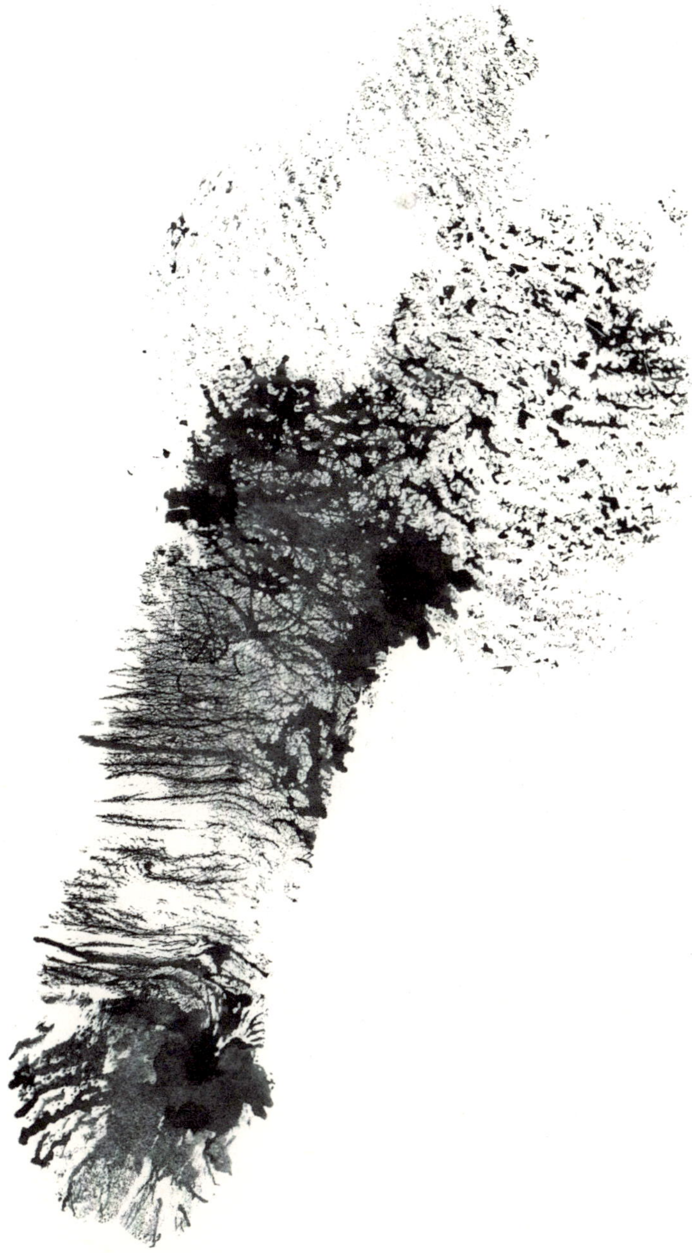

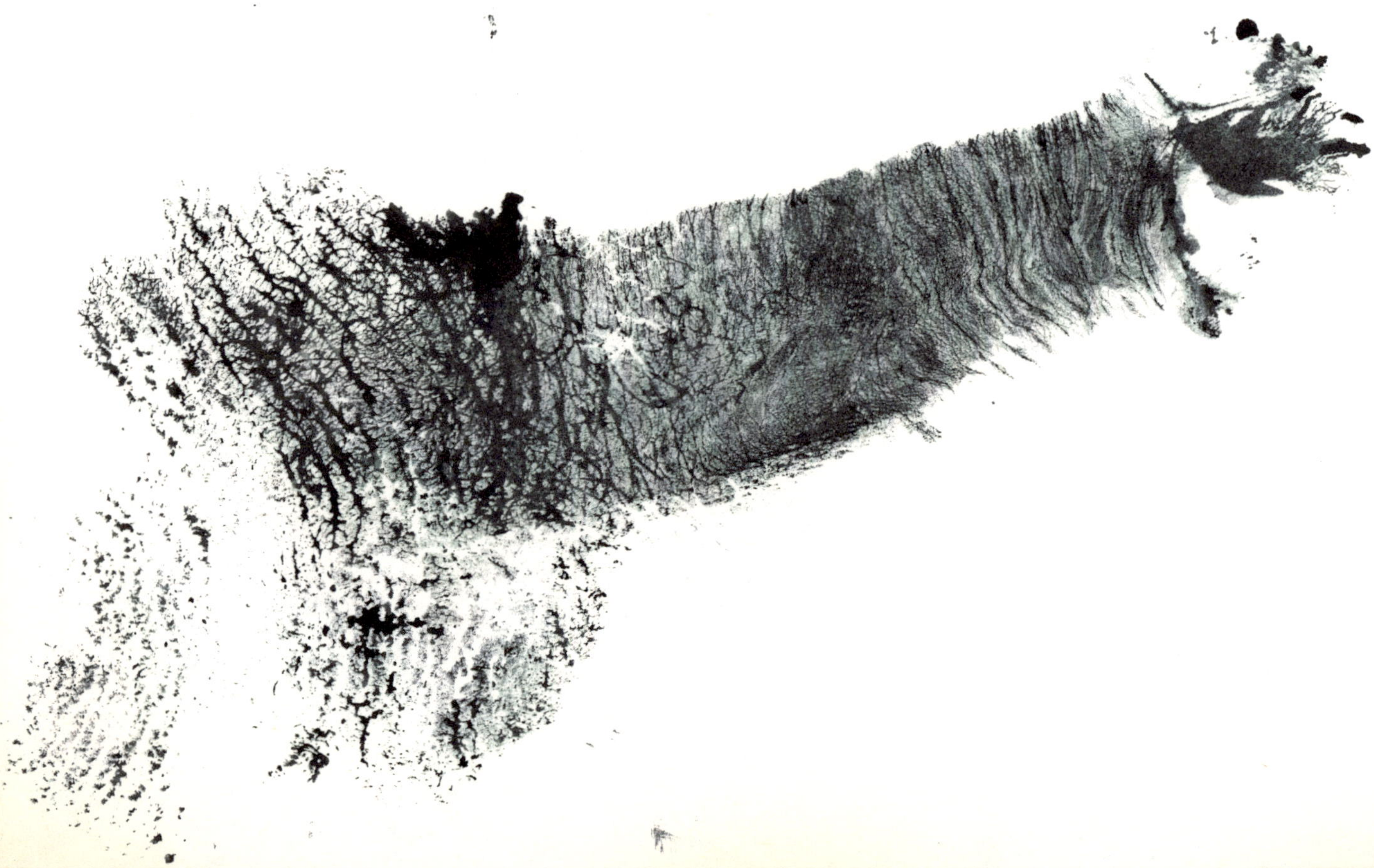

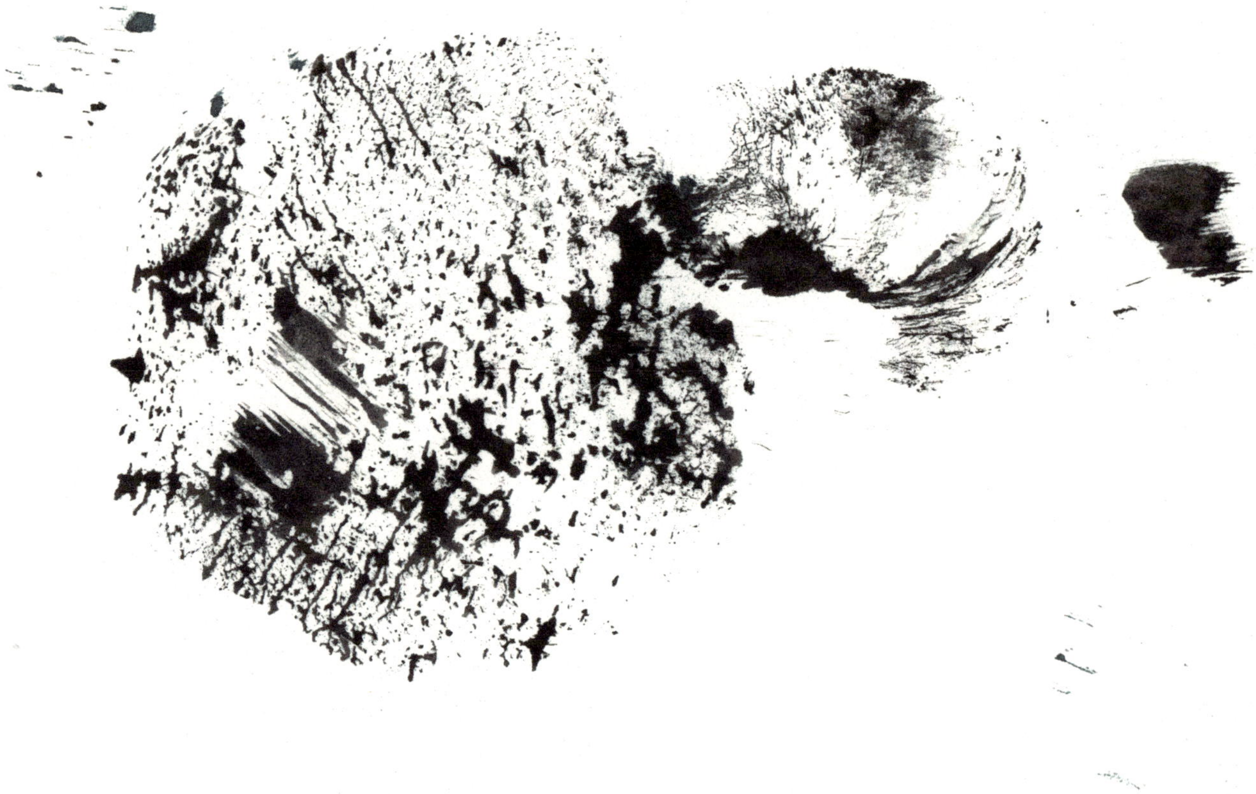

33–48
Master Bet
details
2009

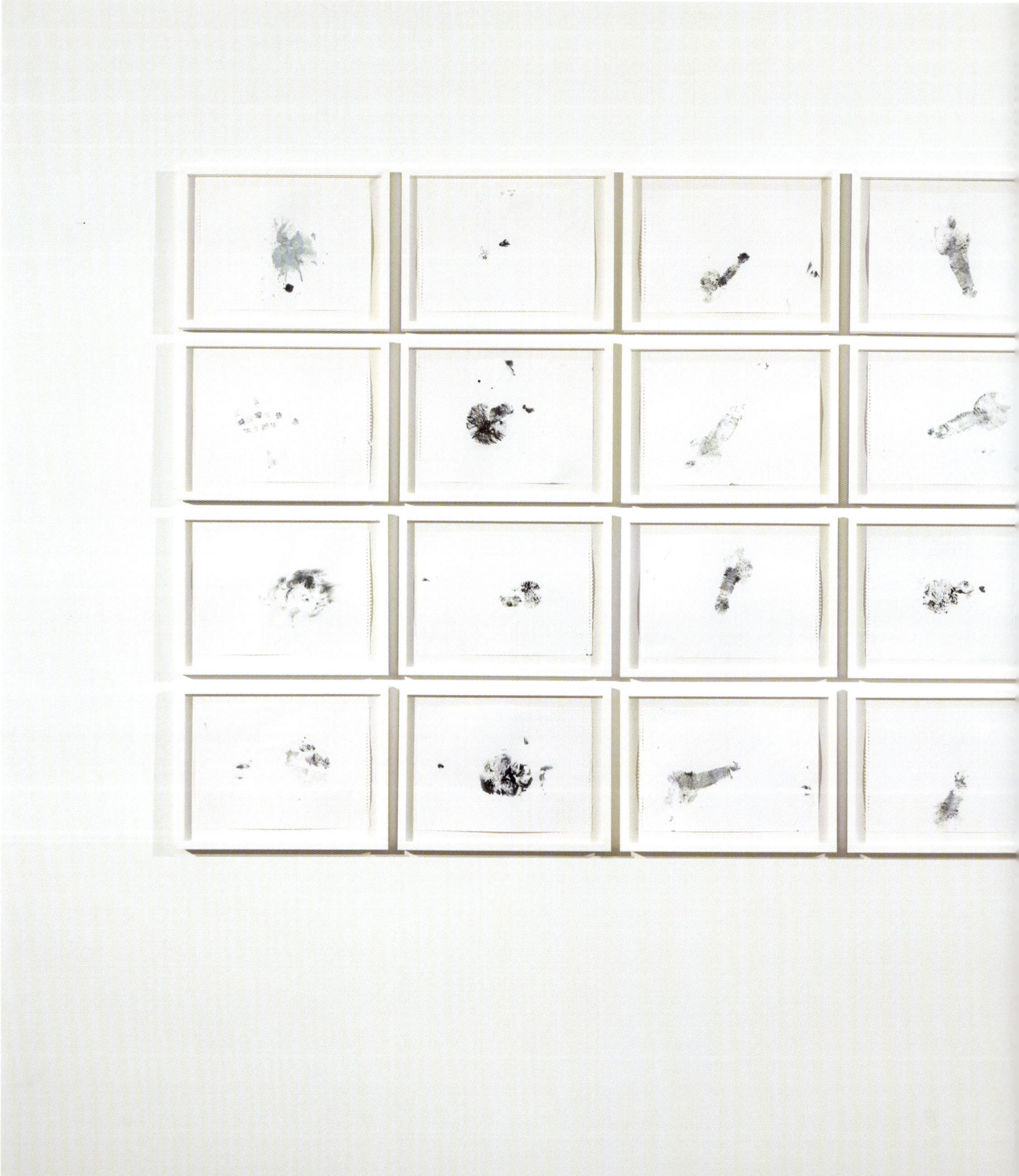

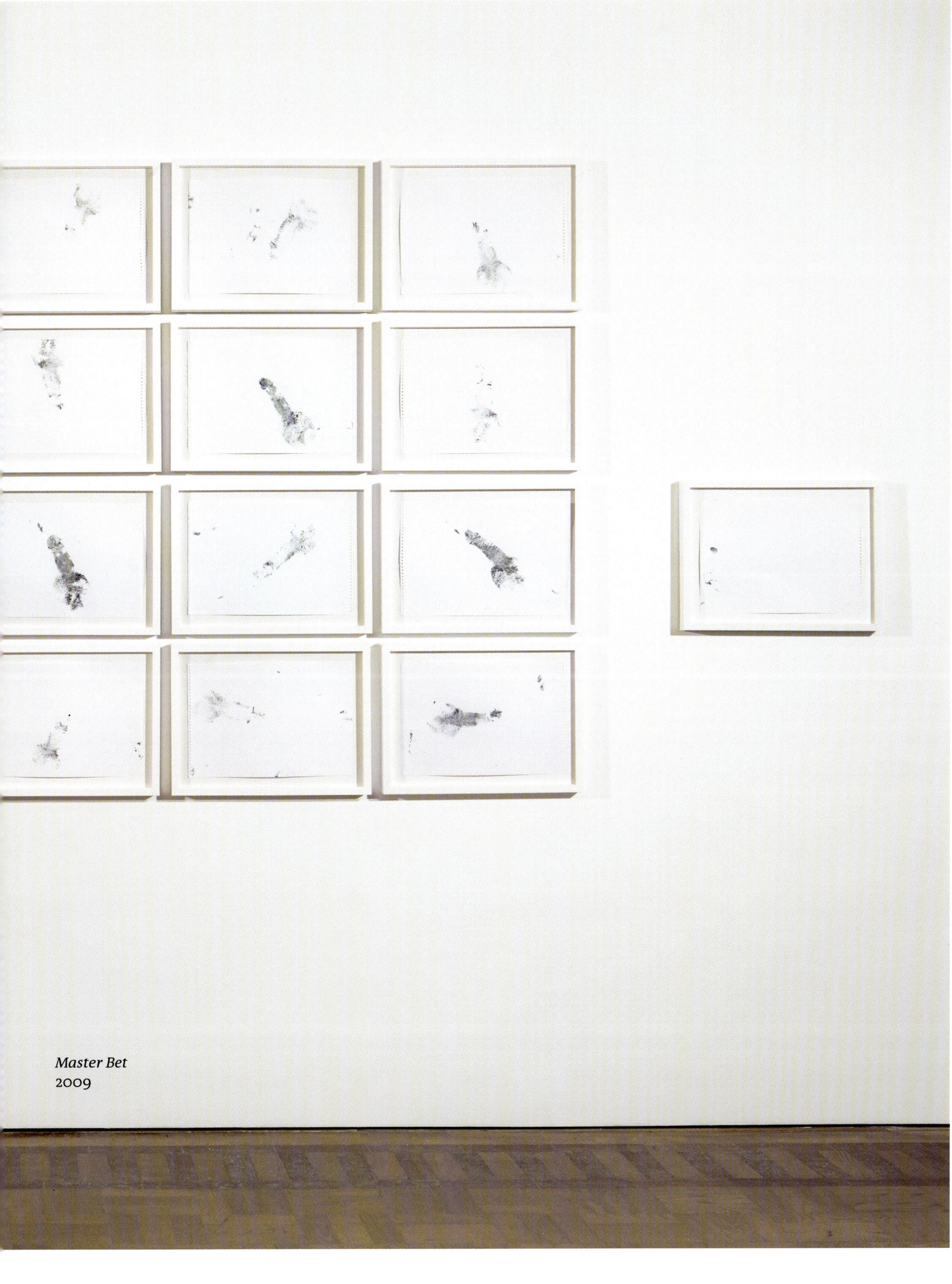

Master Bet
2009

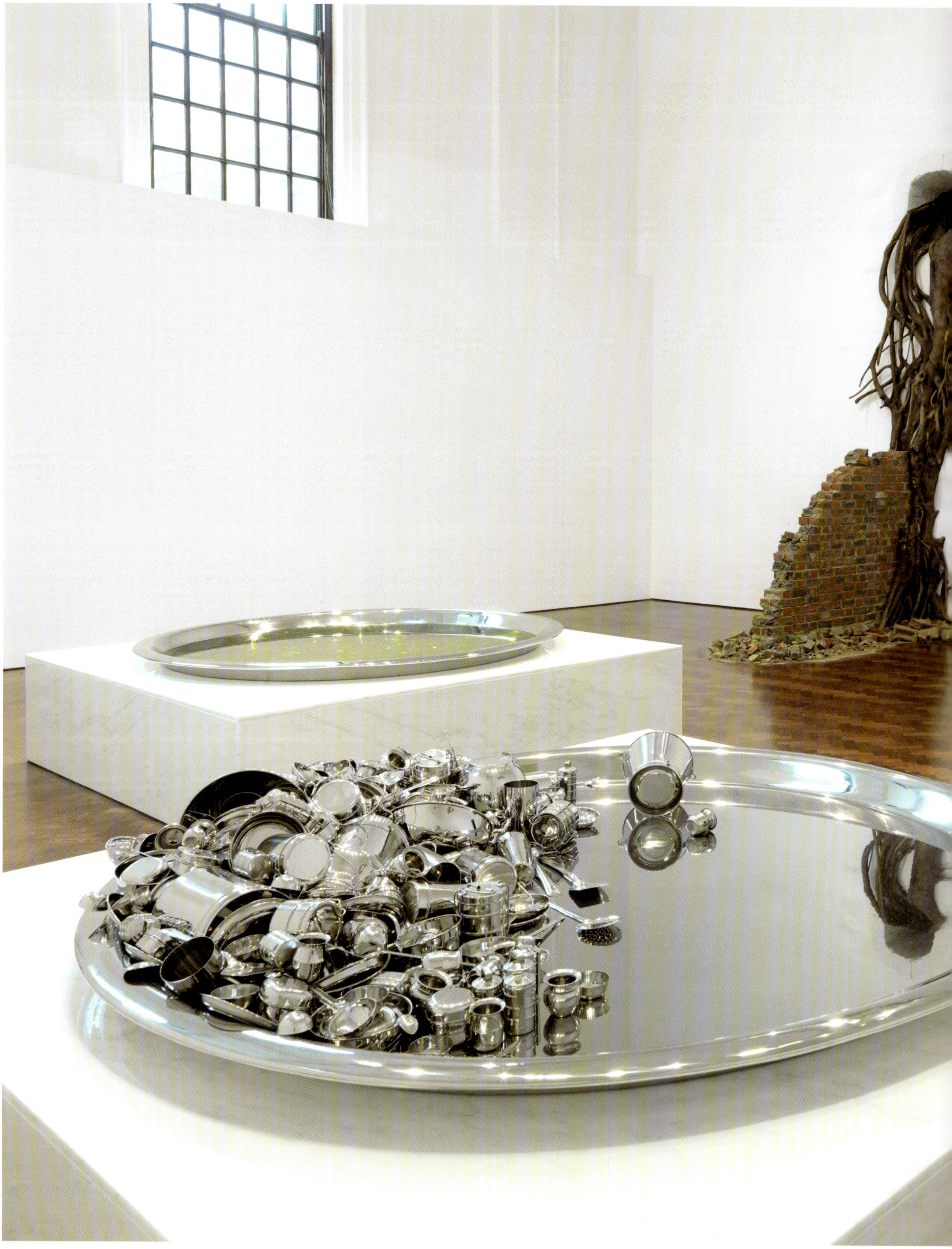

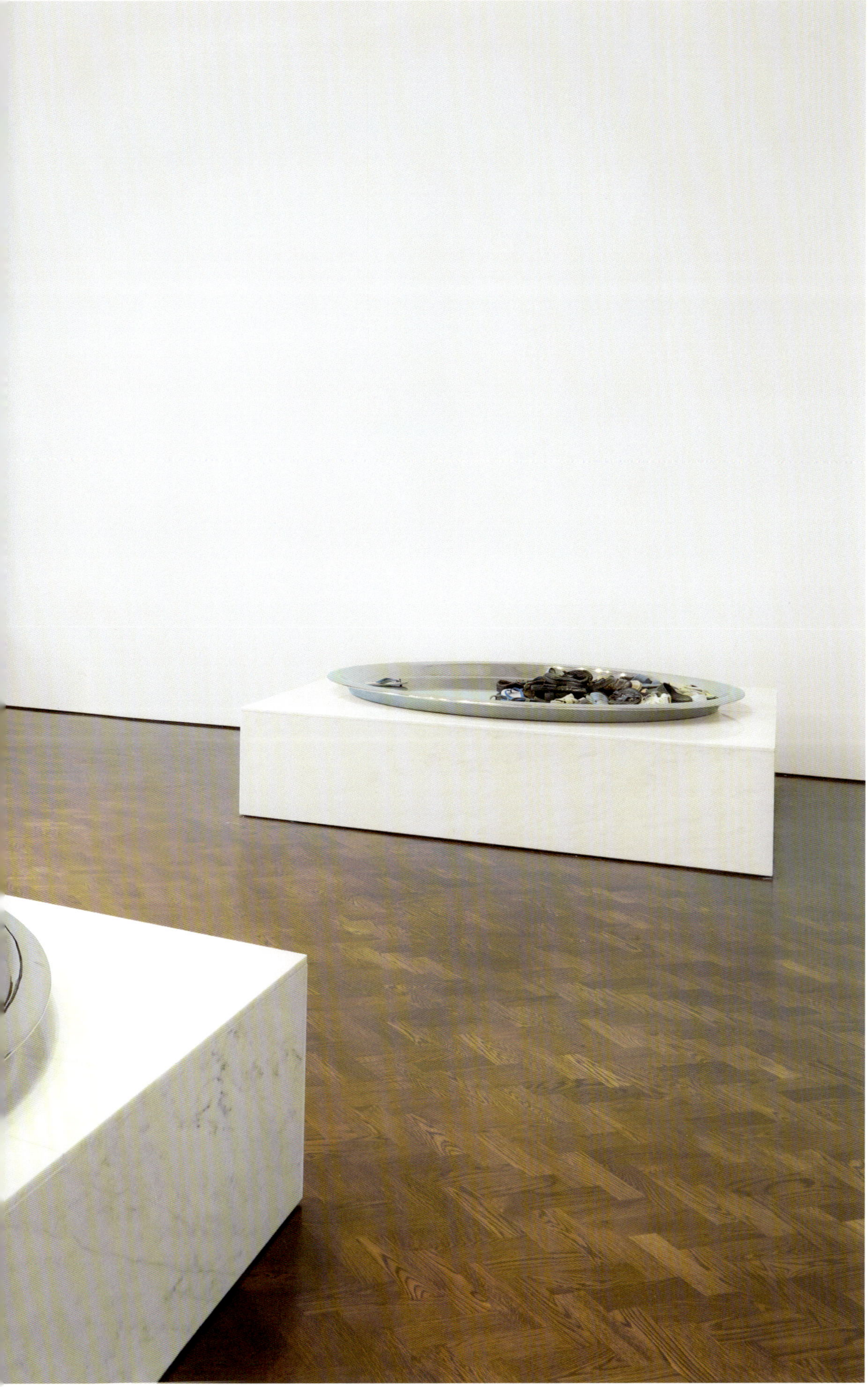

Installation view
Hauser & Wirth London
2009

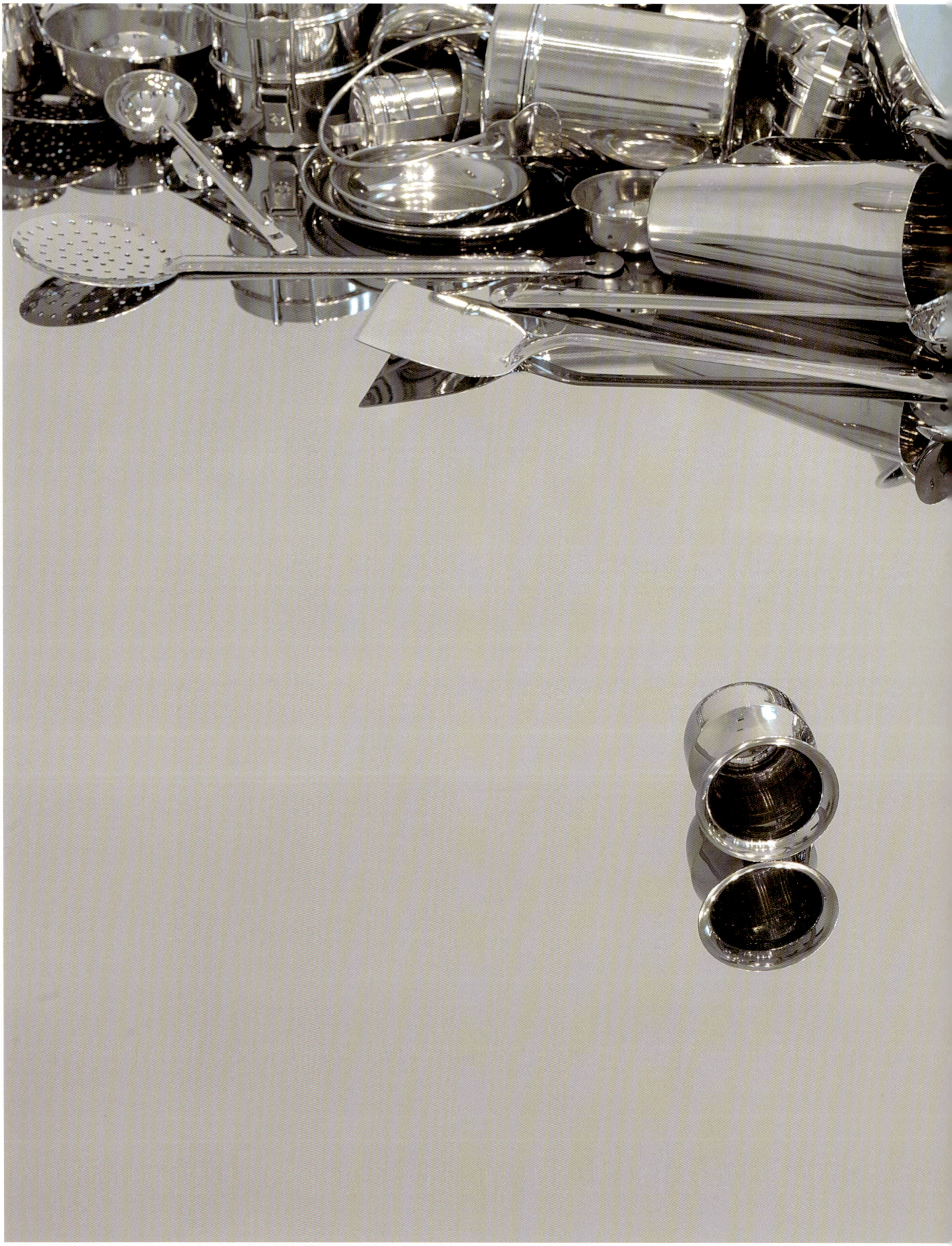

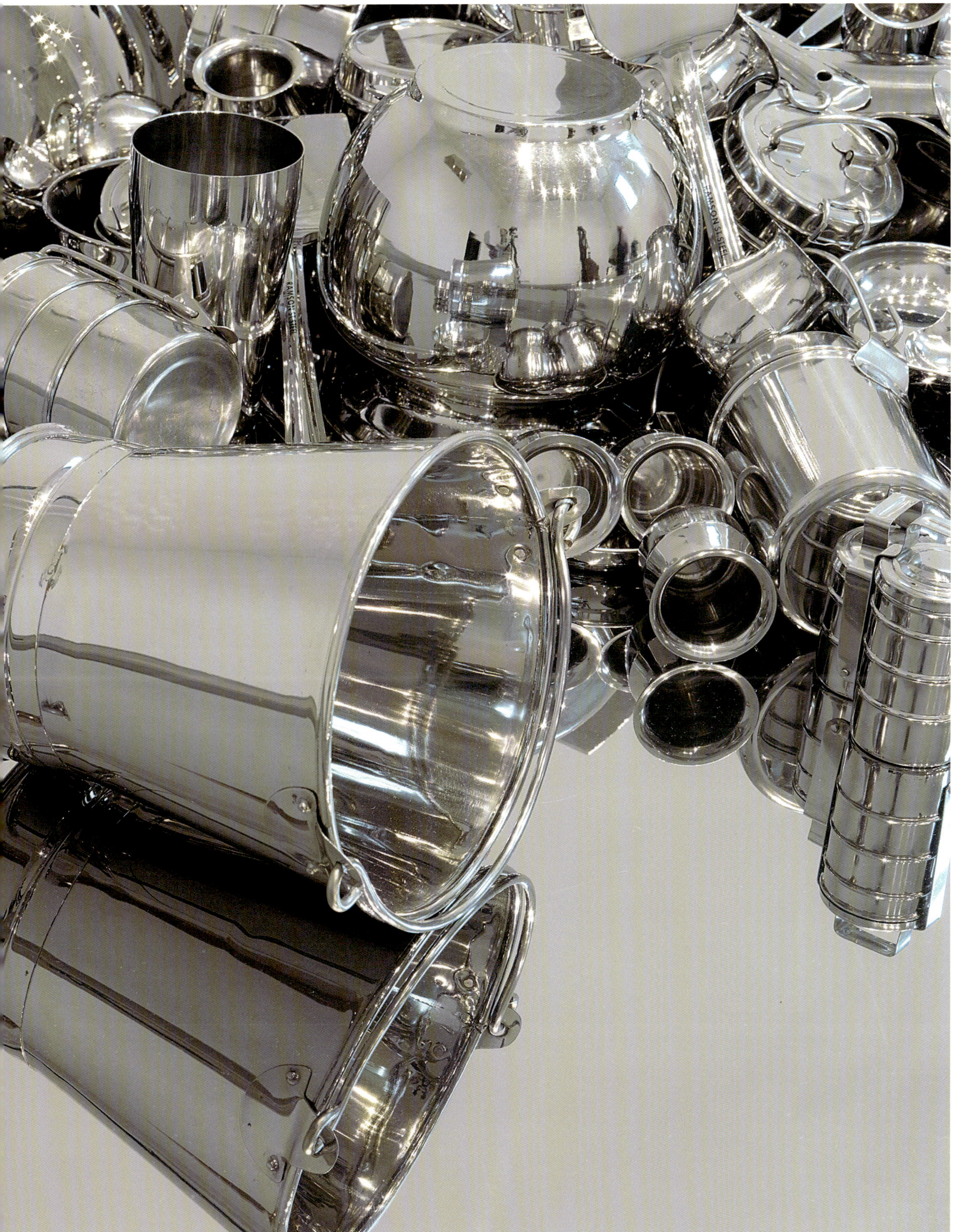

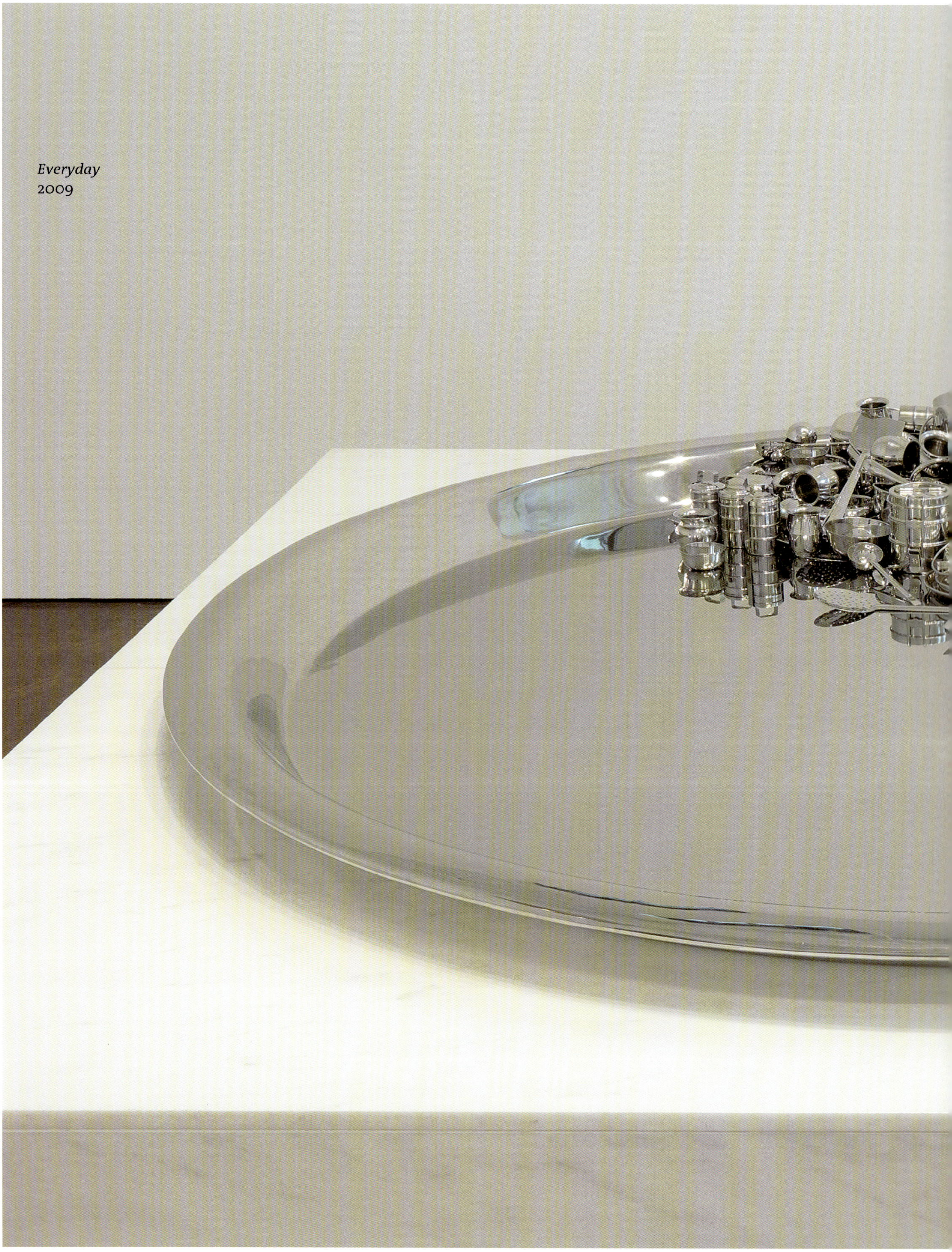

Everyday
2009

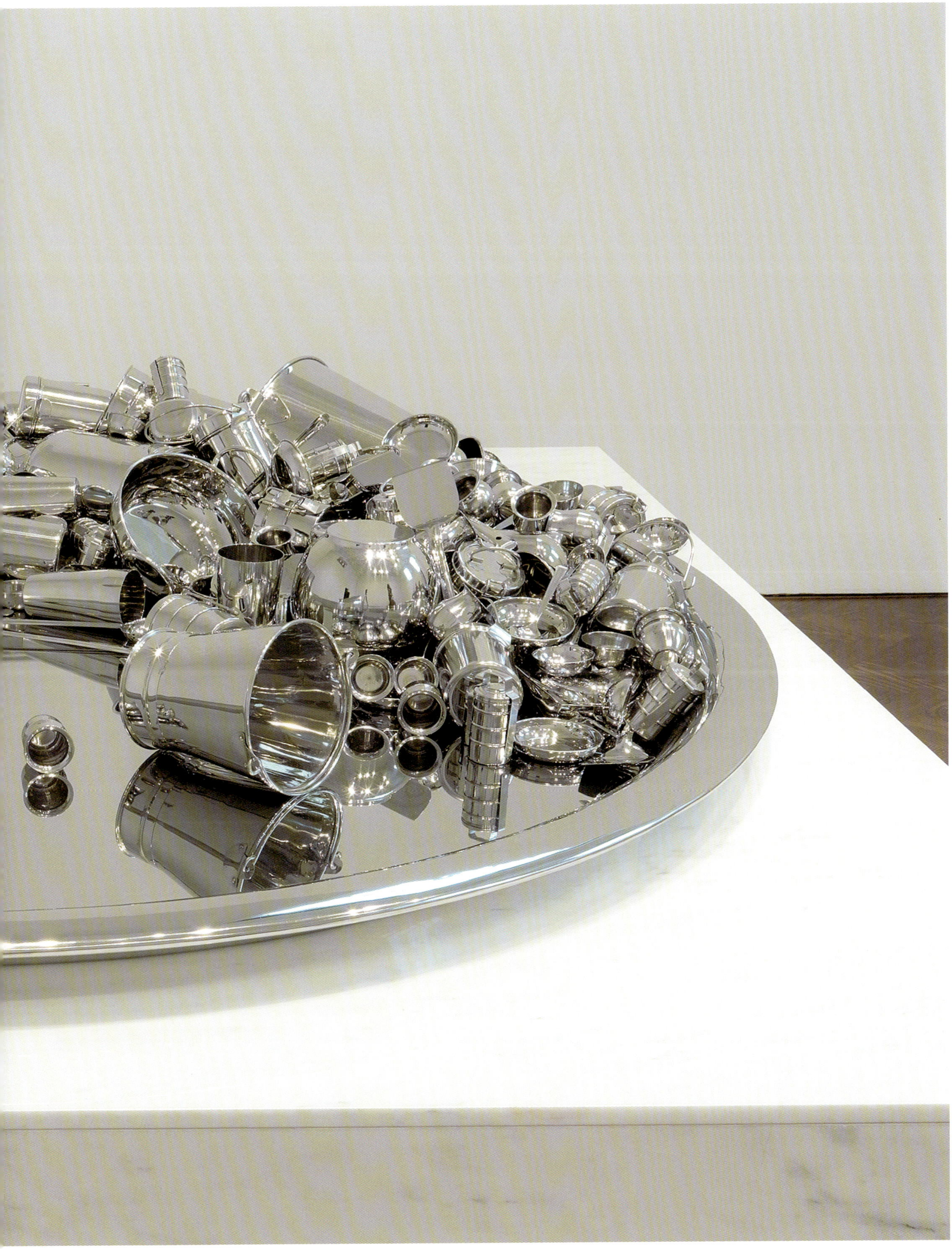

A Penny for Belief II
2009

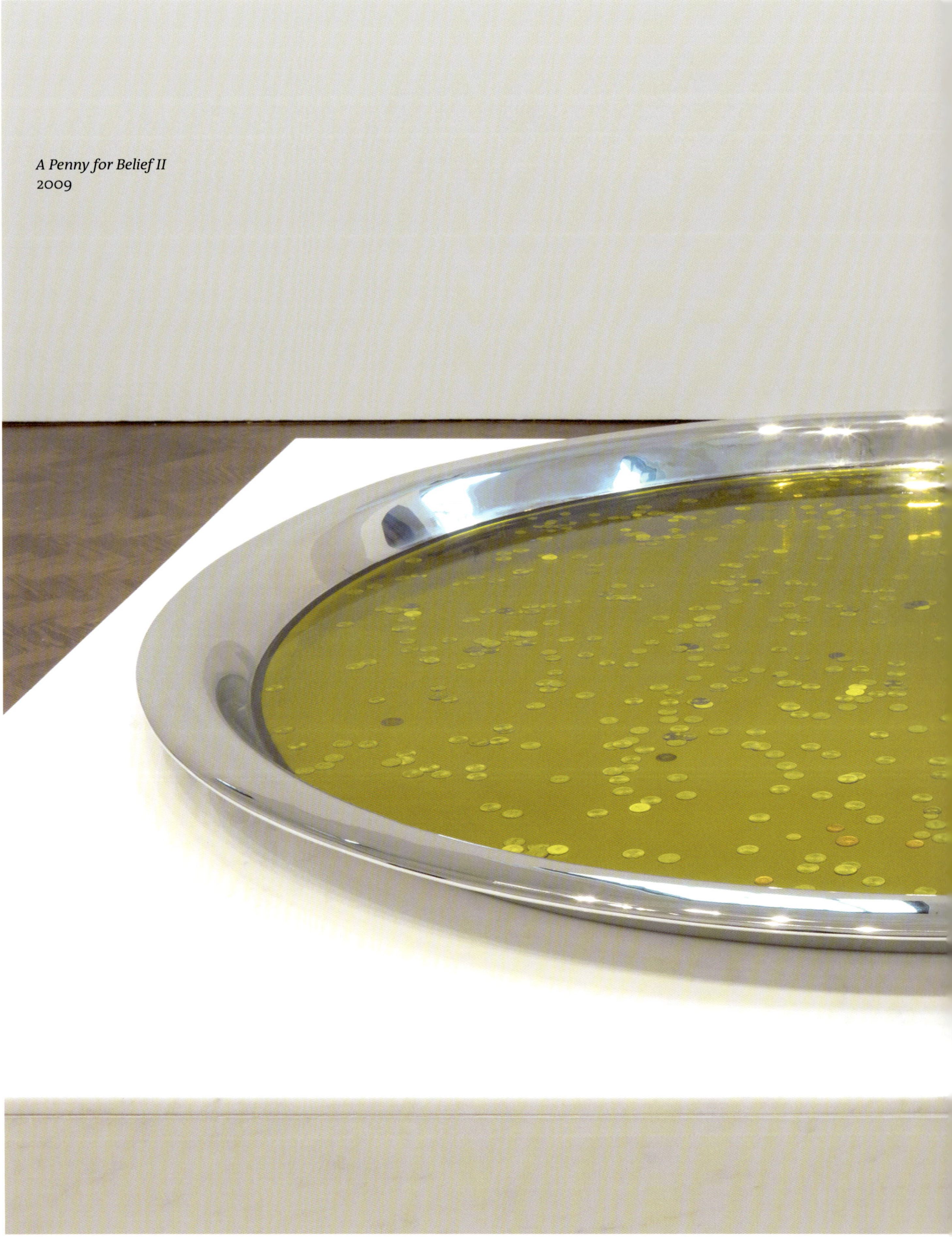

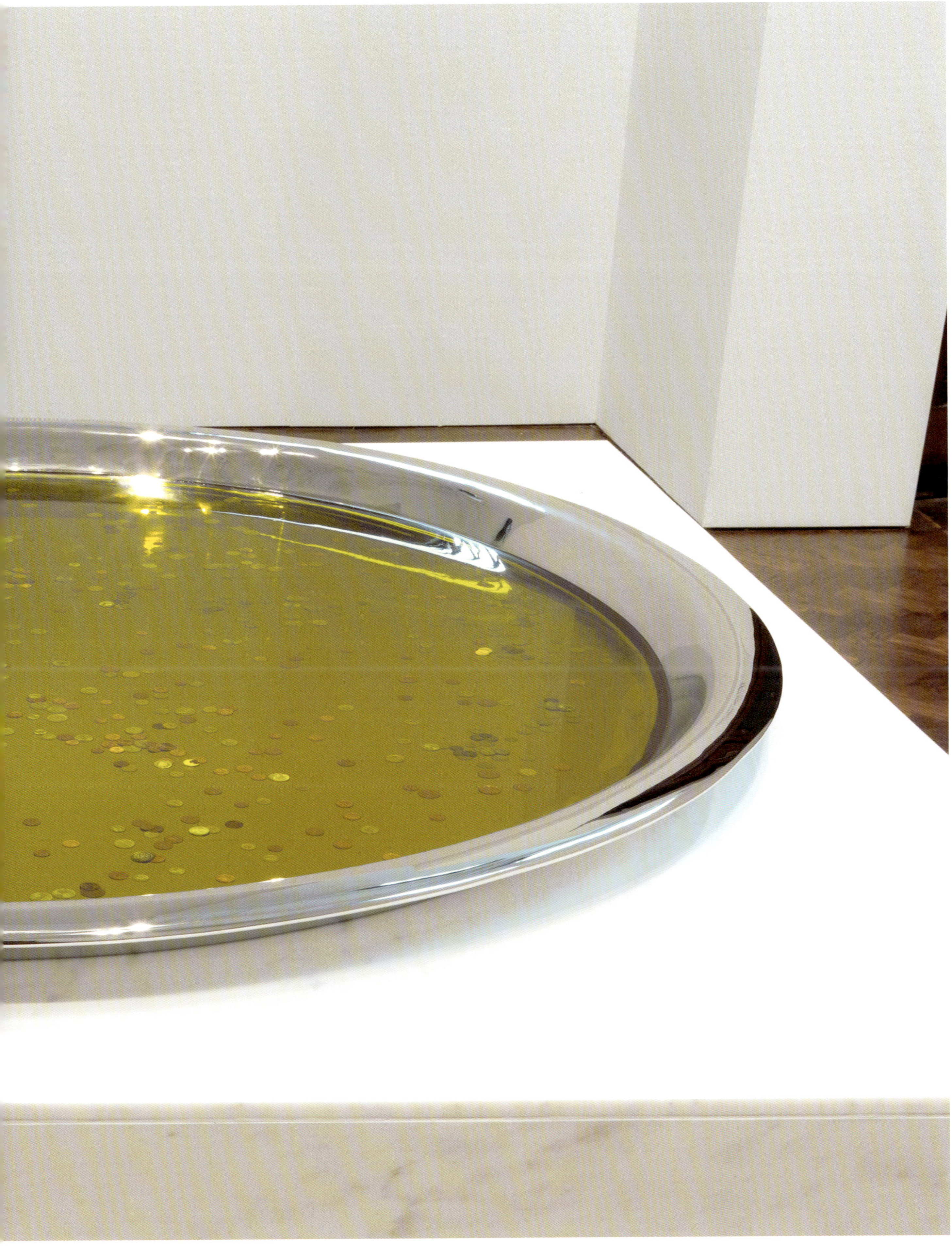

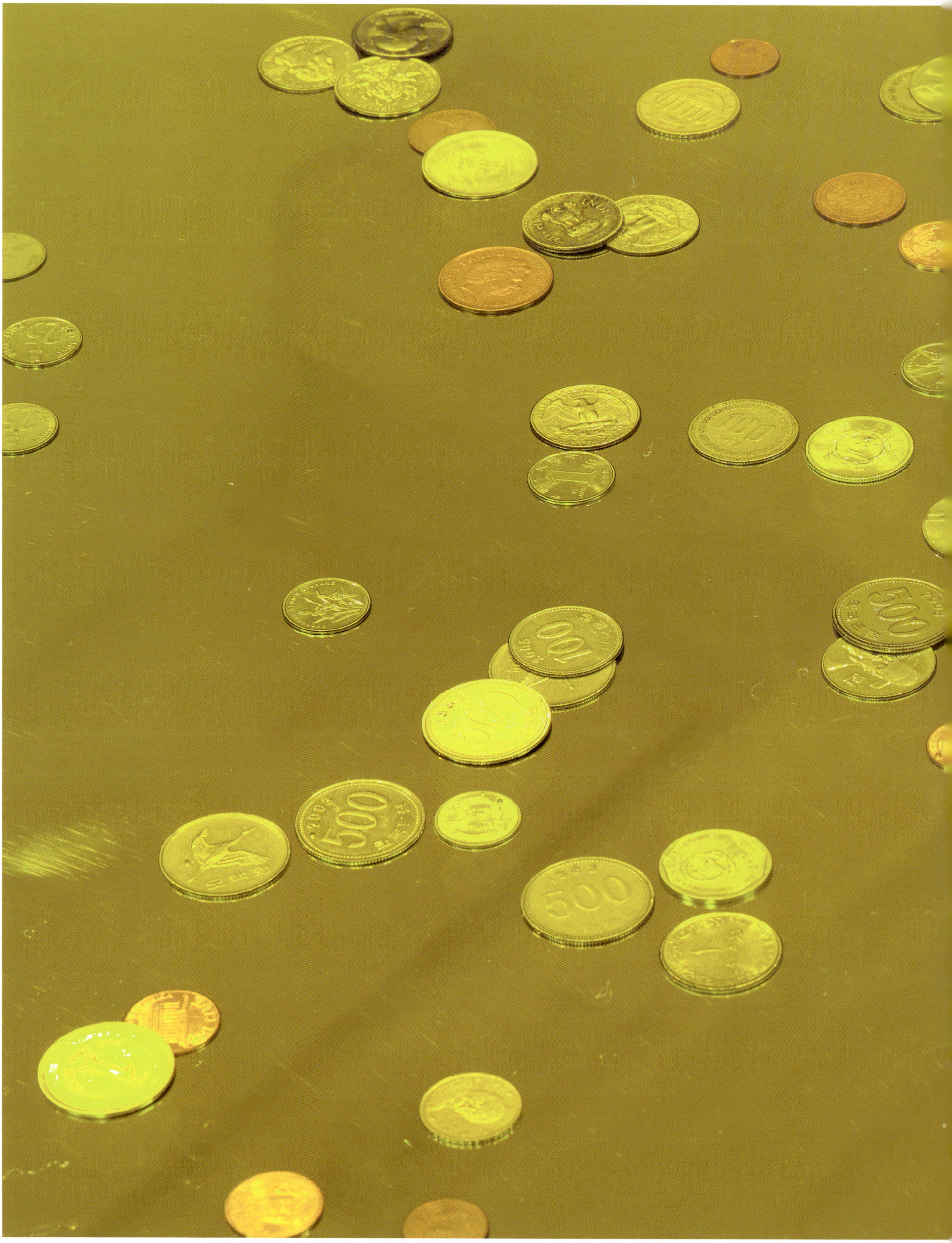

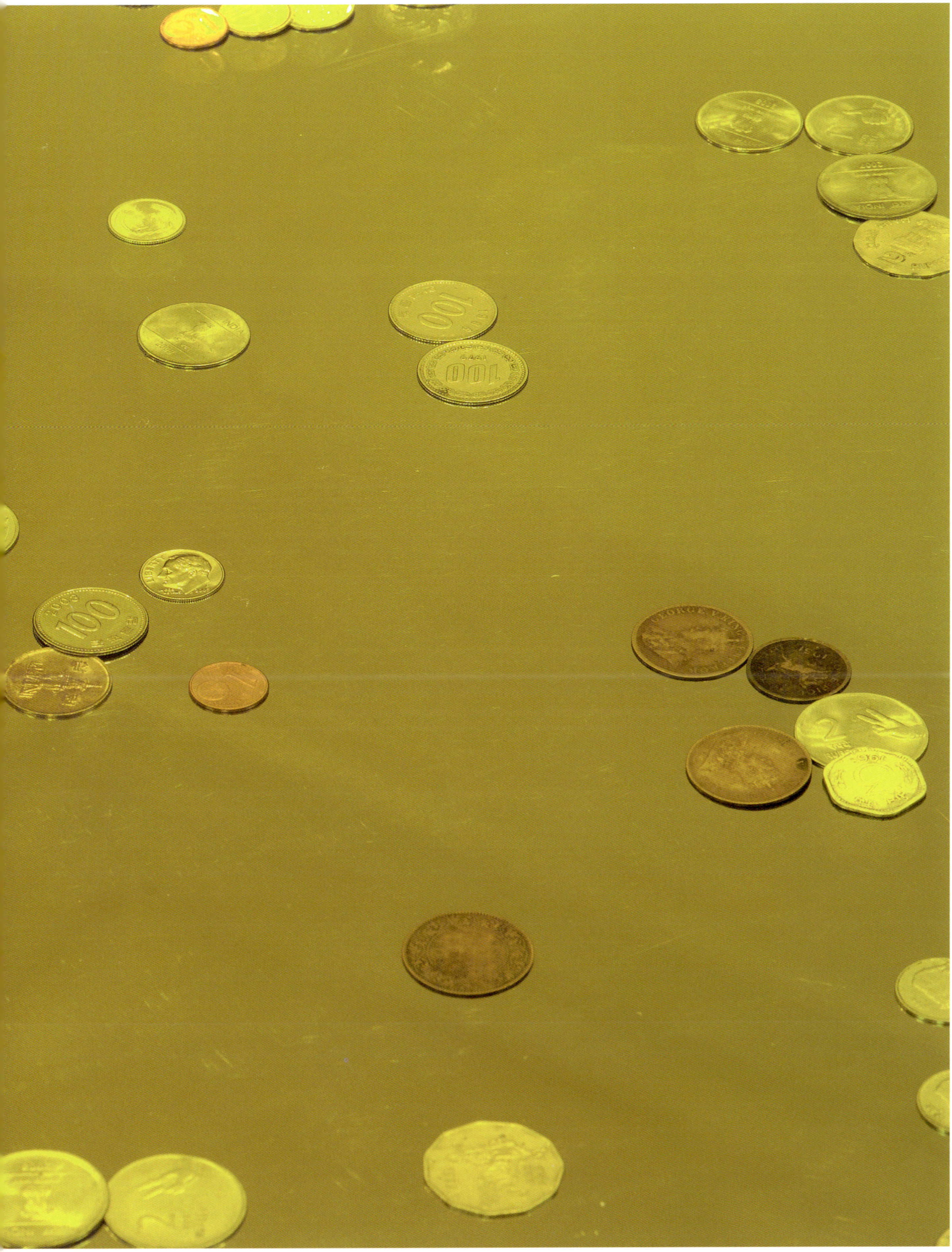

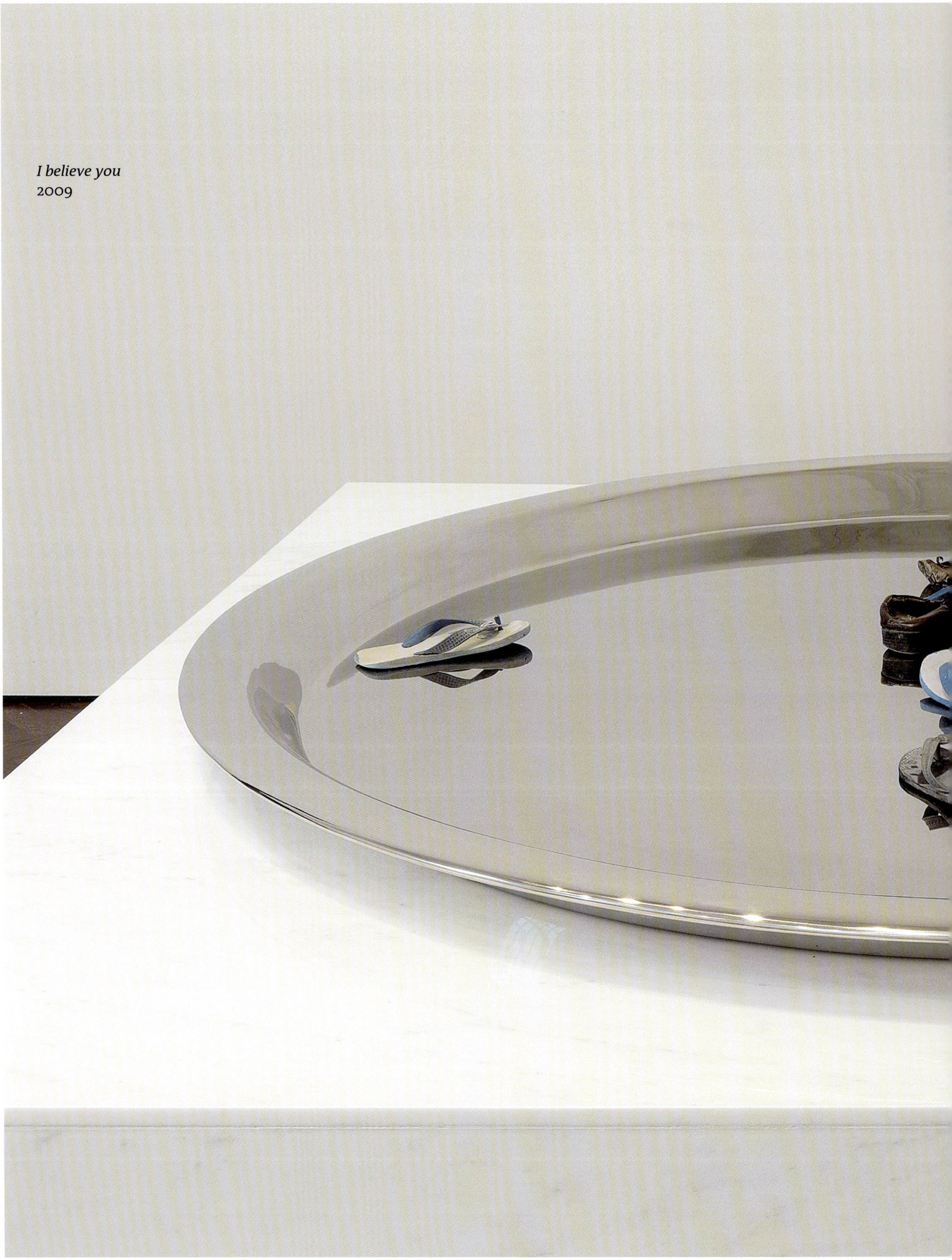

I believe you
2009

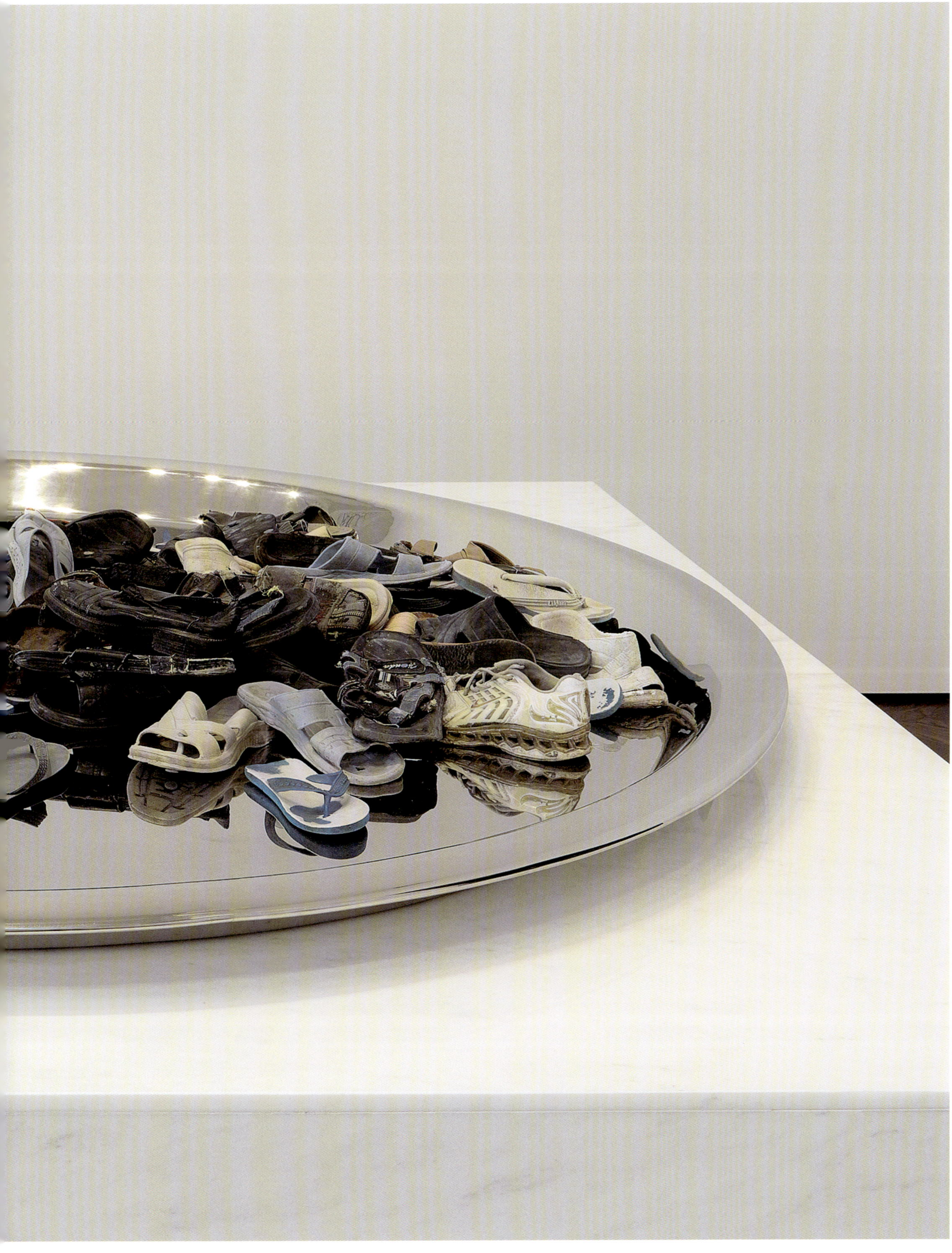

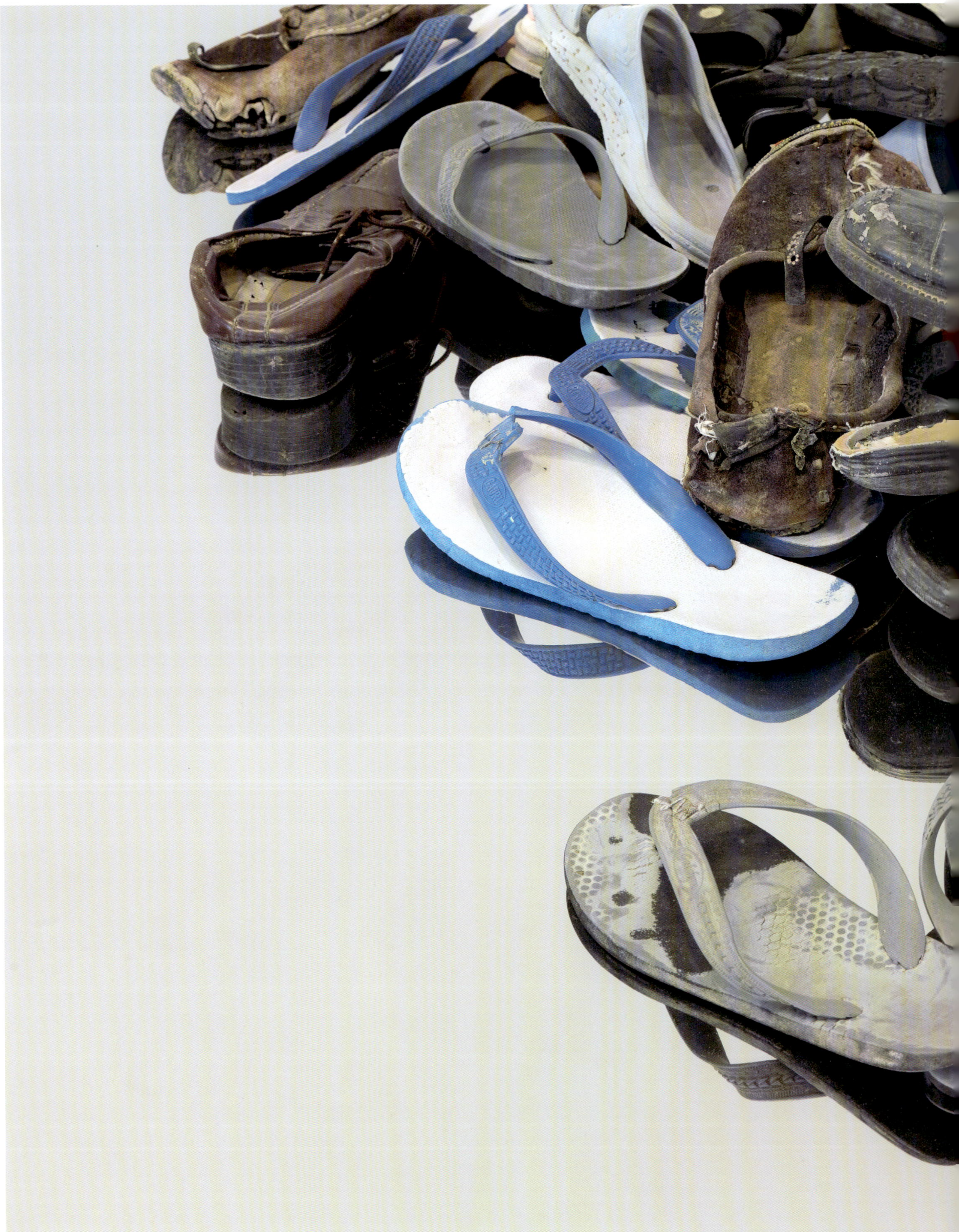

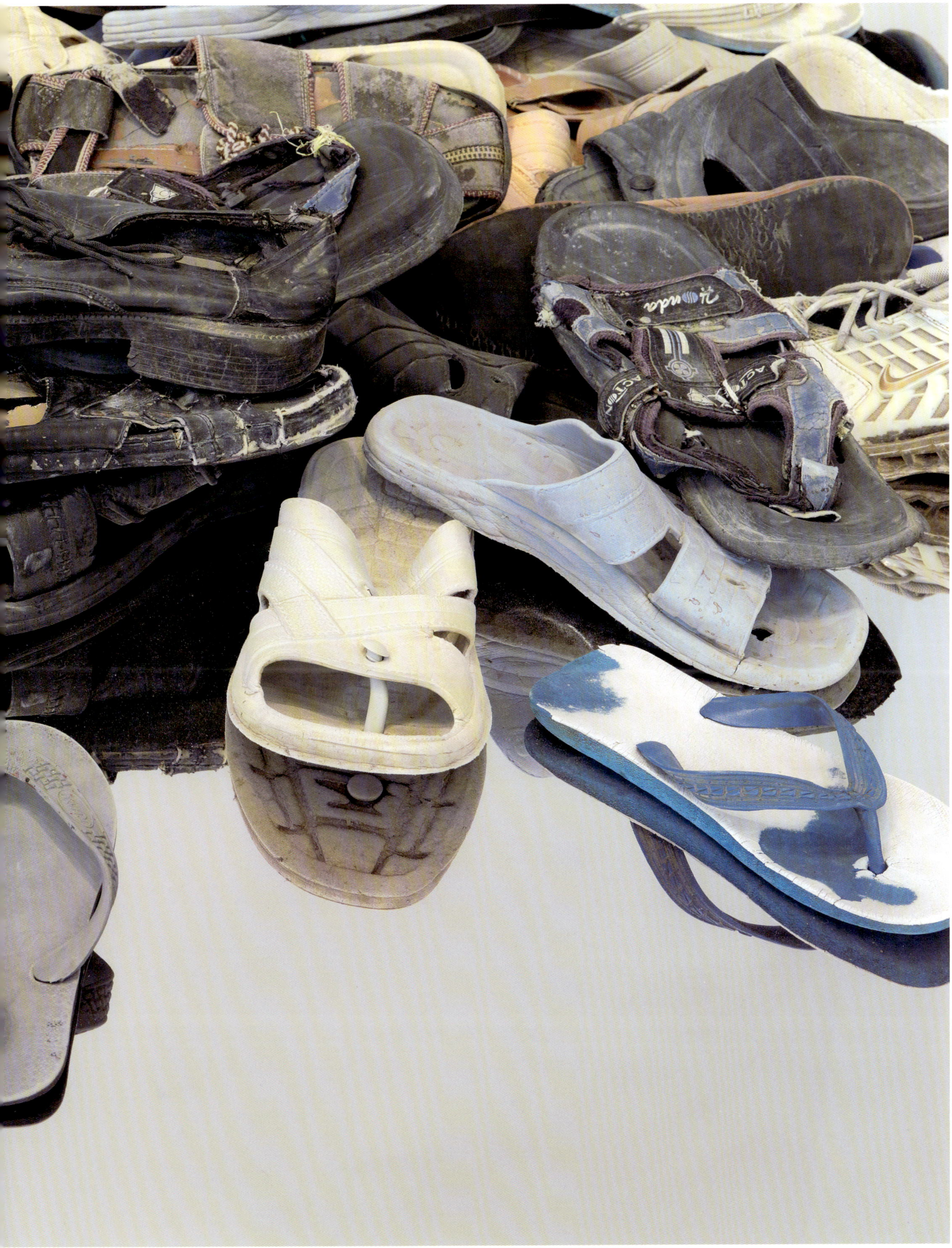

Wall
2009

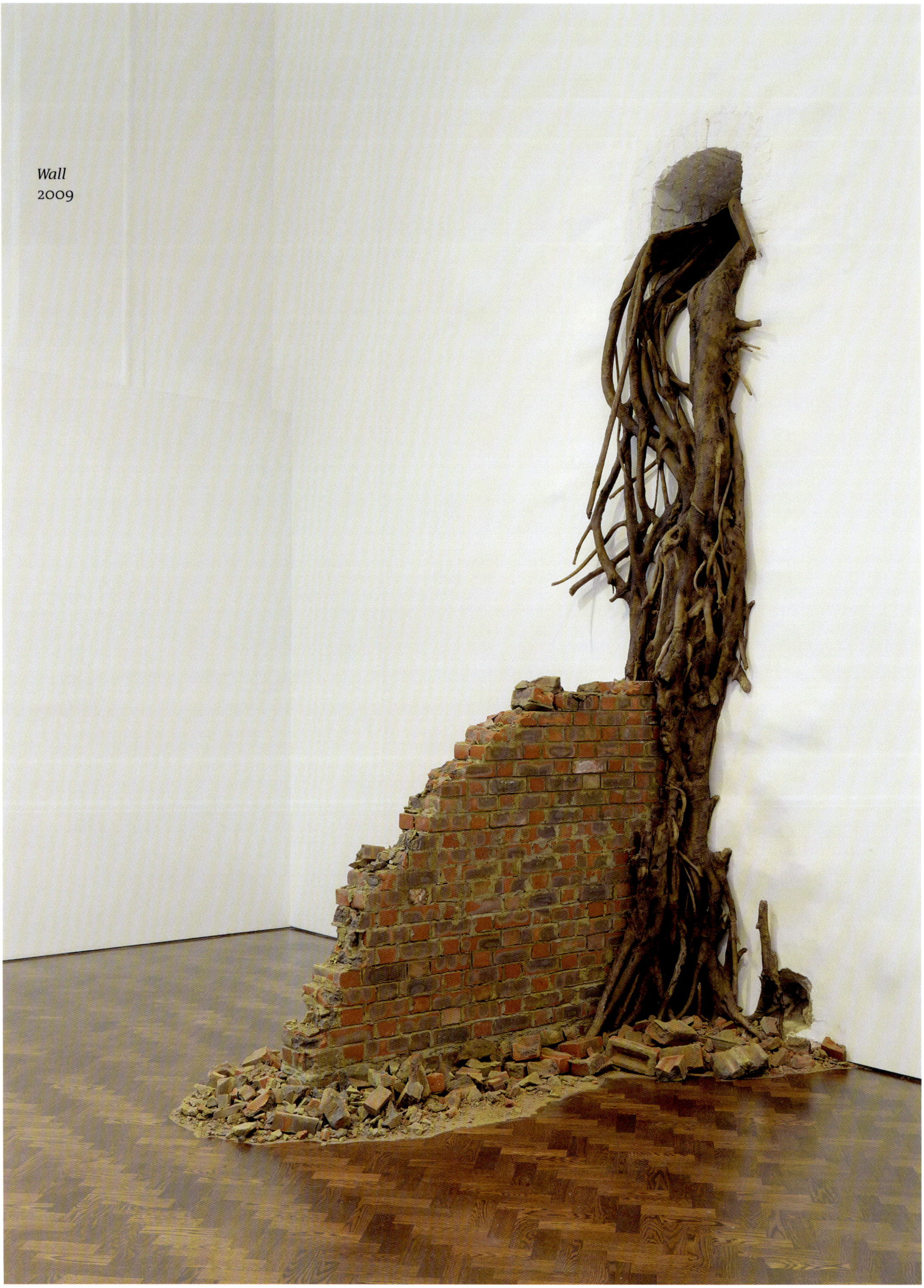

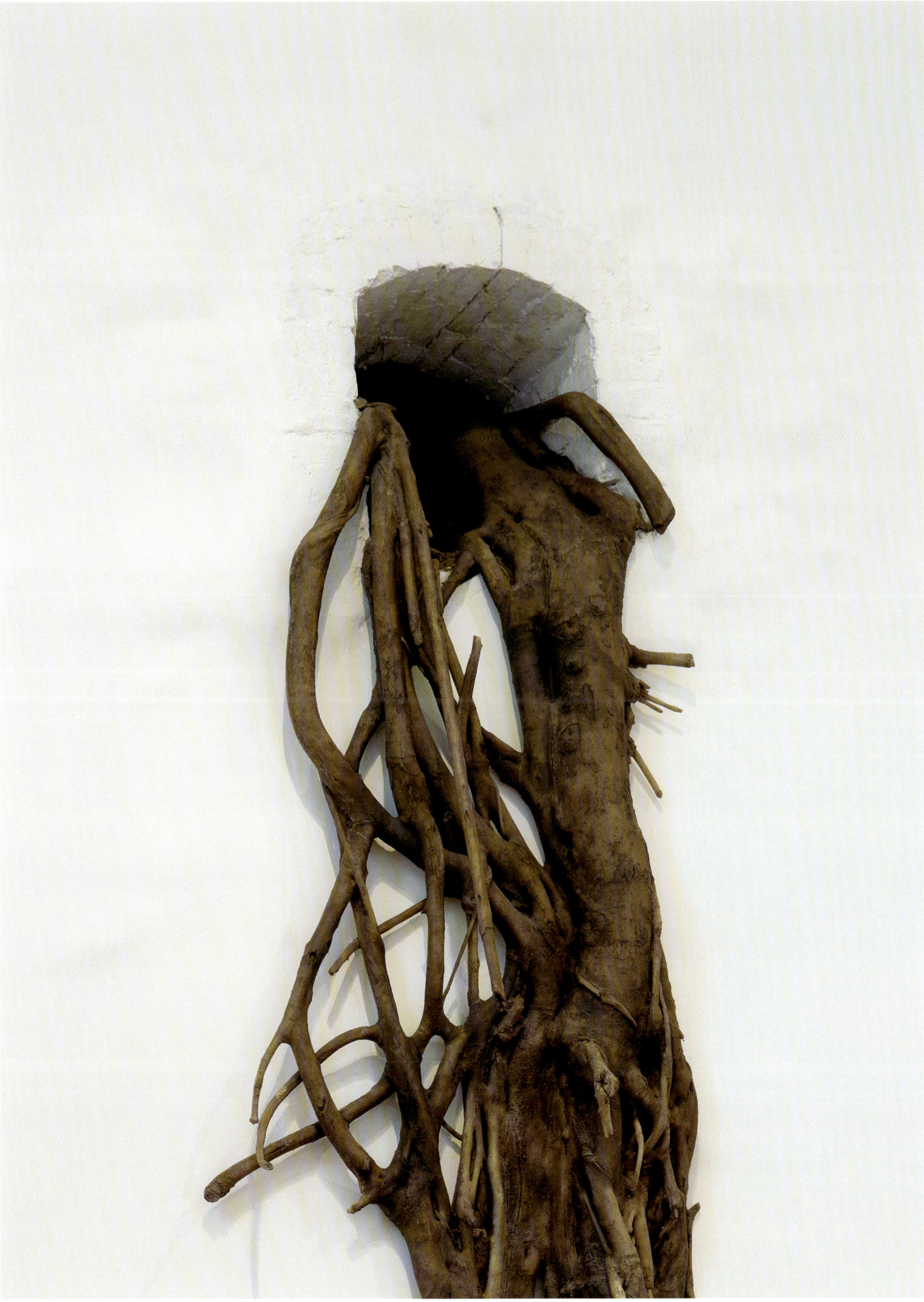

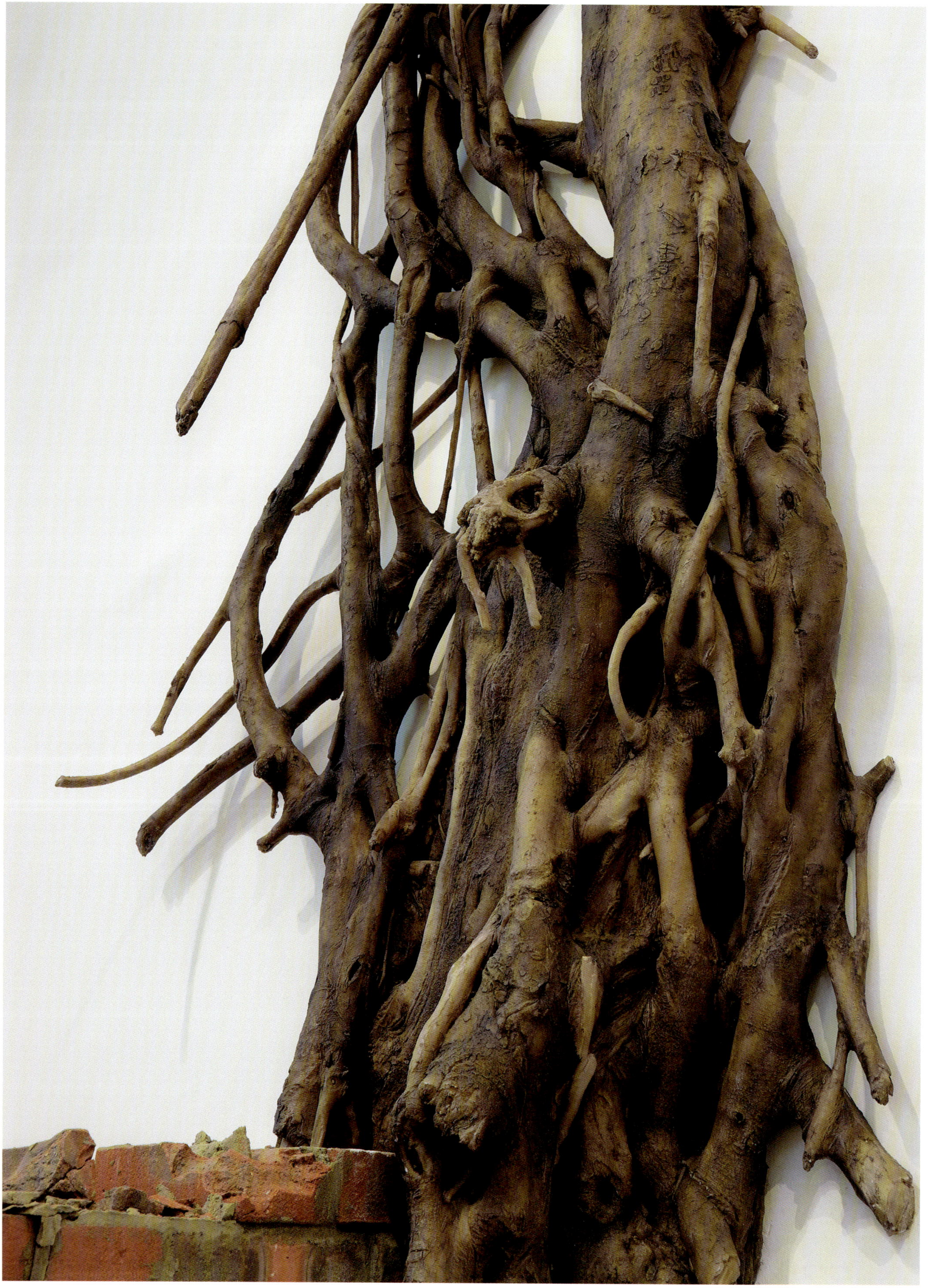

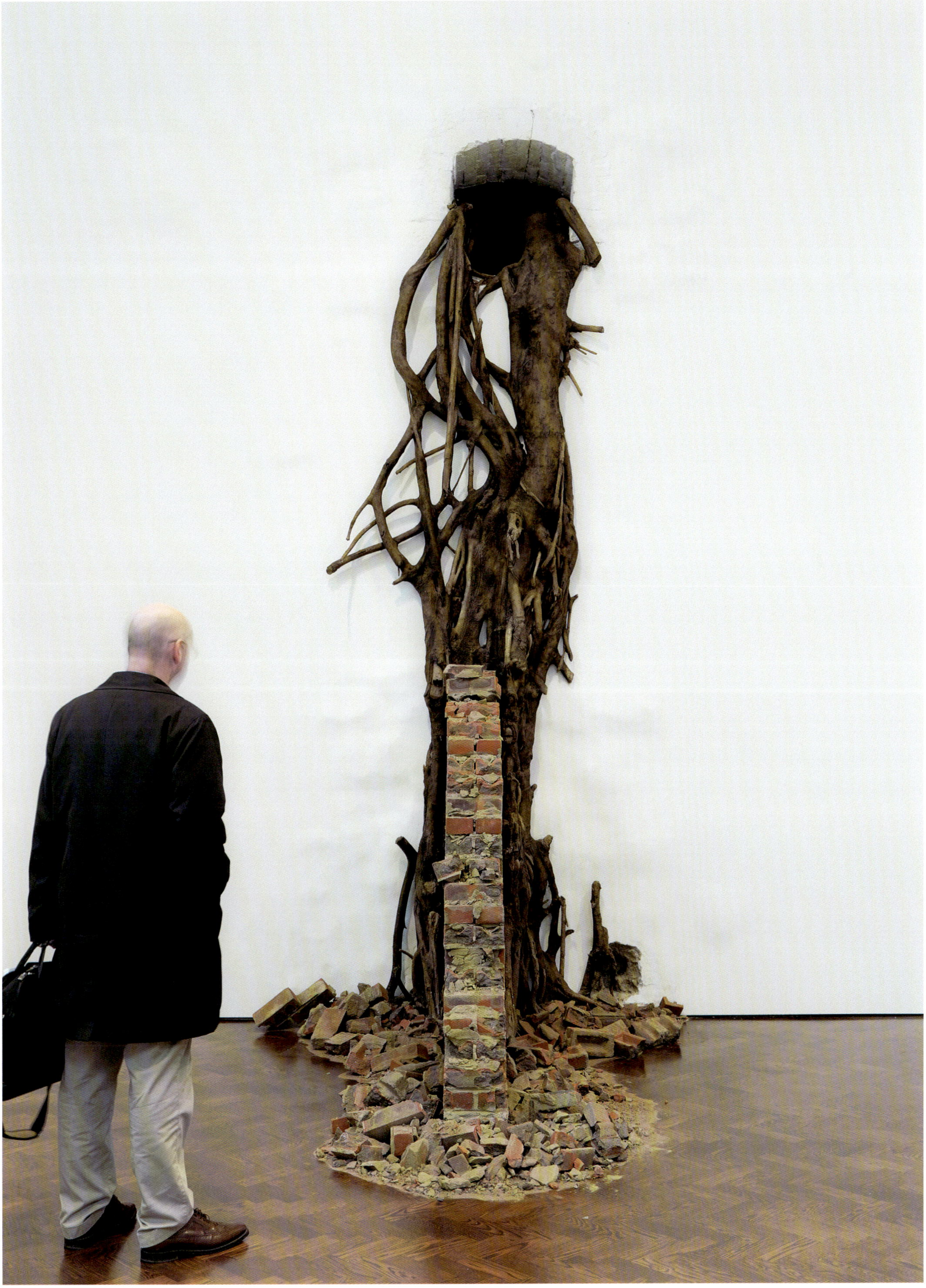

Installation view
Hauser & Wirth London
2009

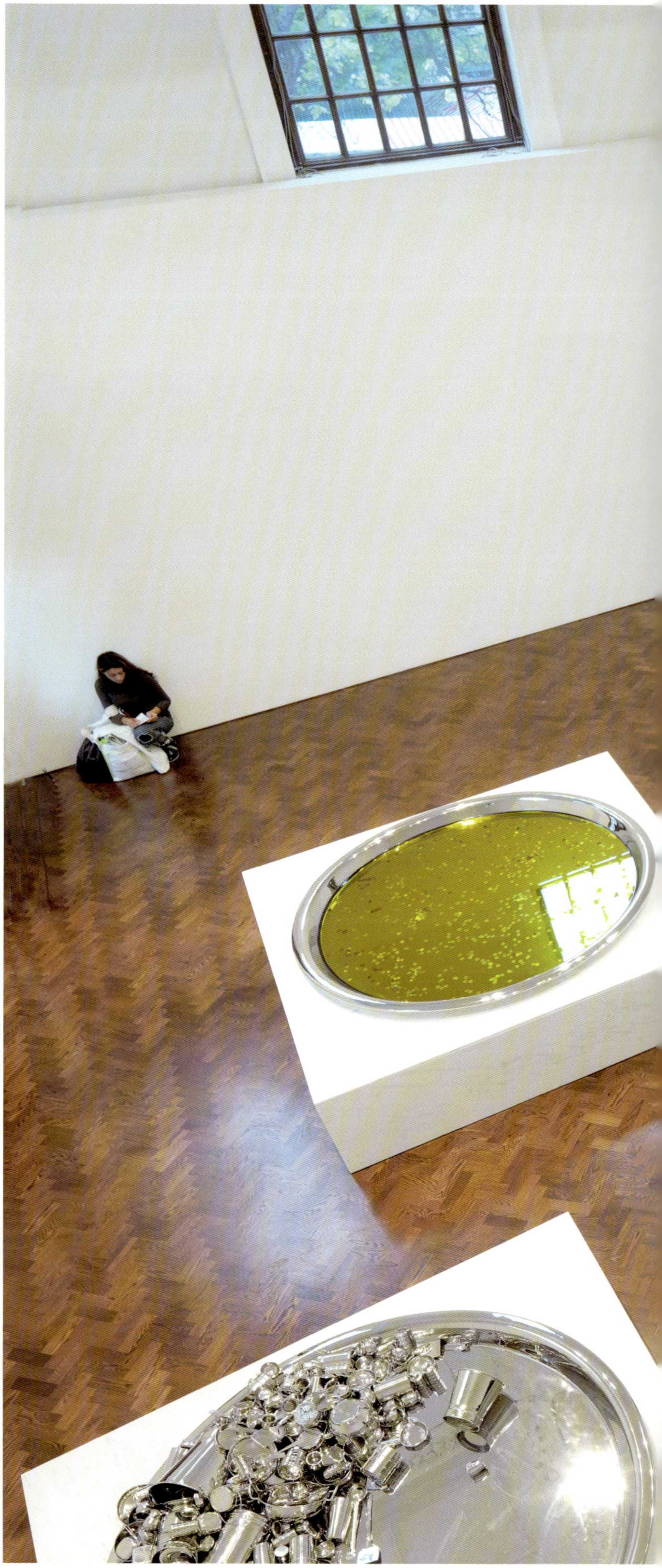

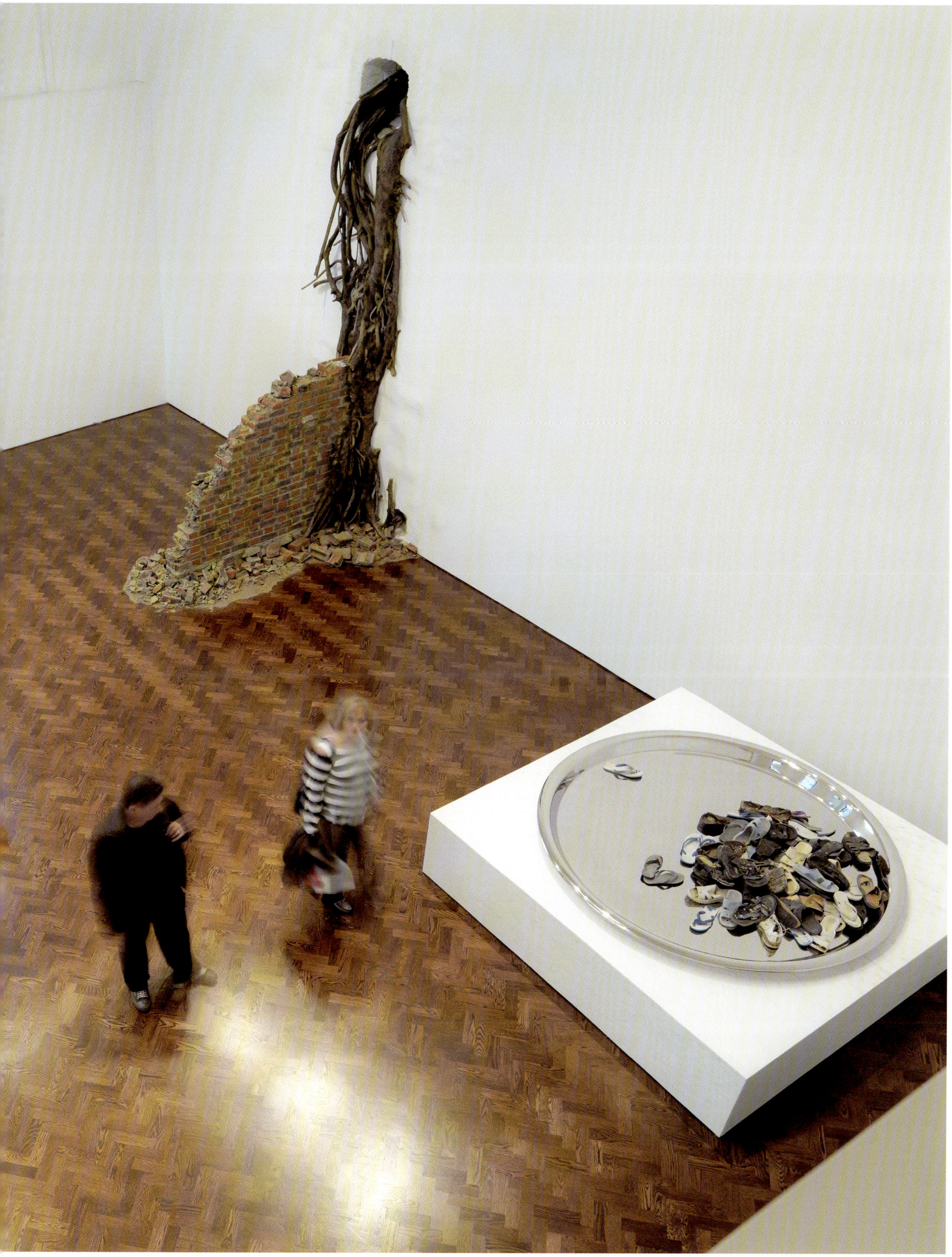

Installation view
Hauser & Wirth London
2009

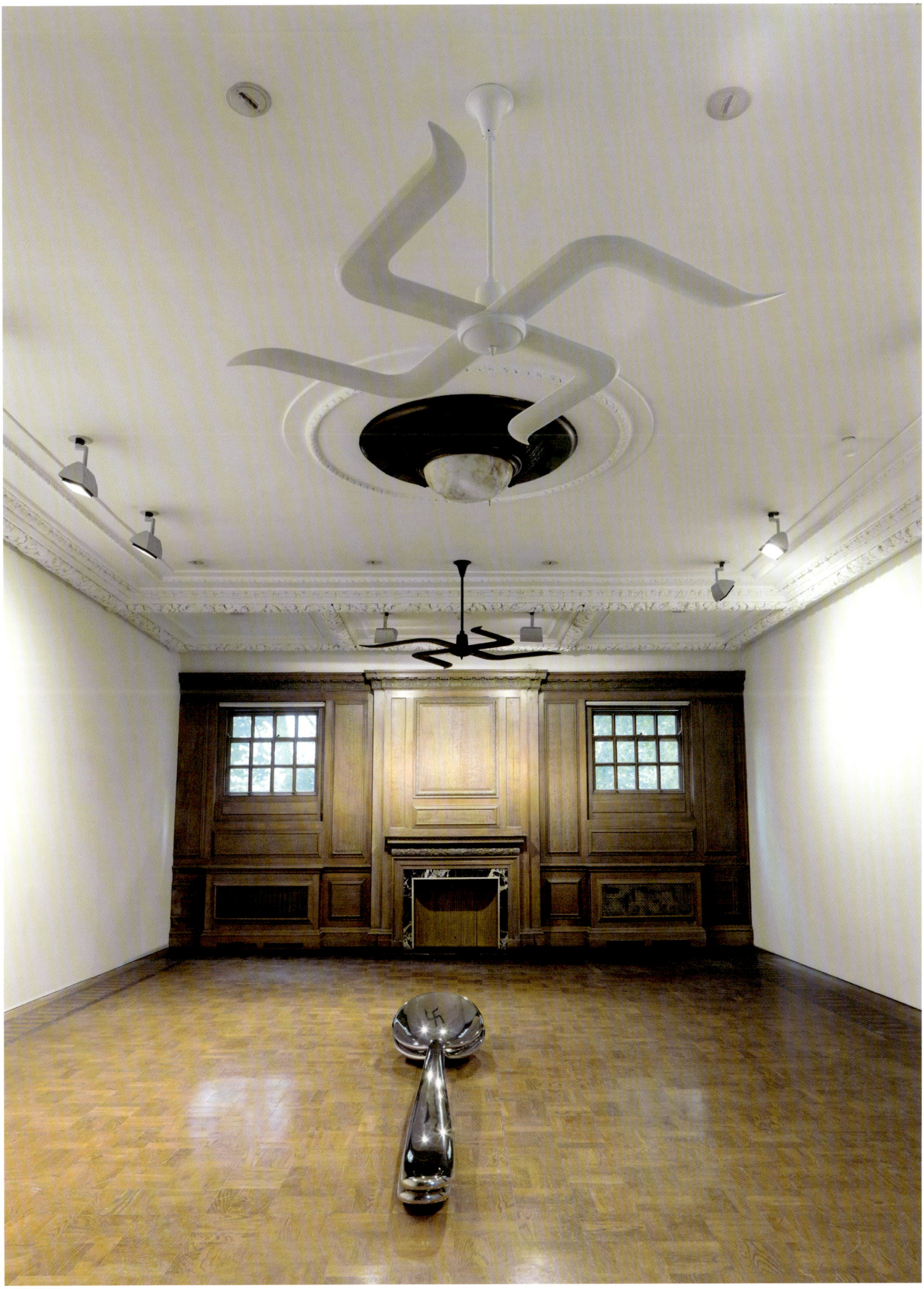

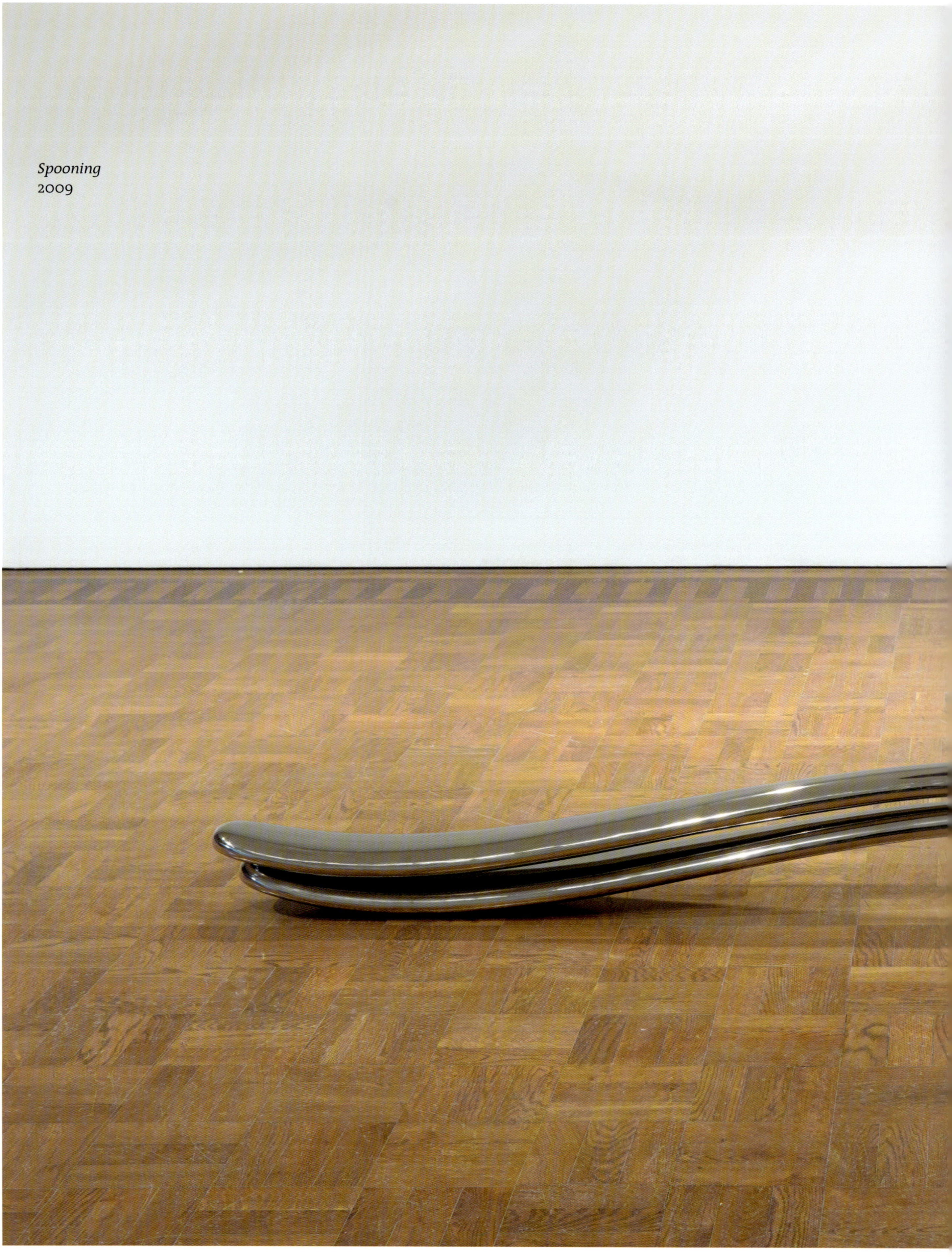

Spooning
2009

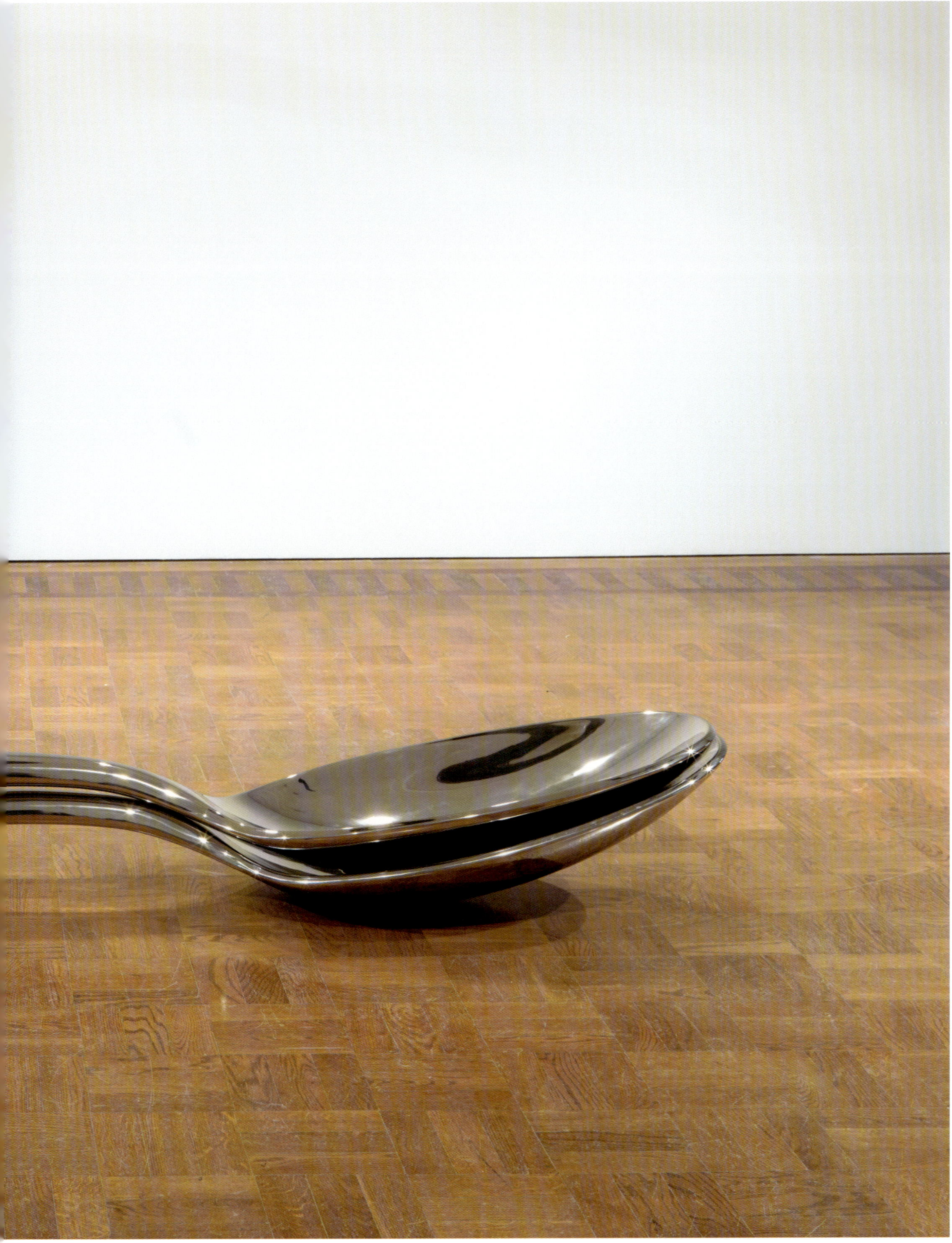

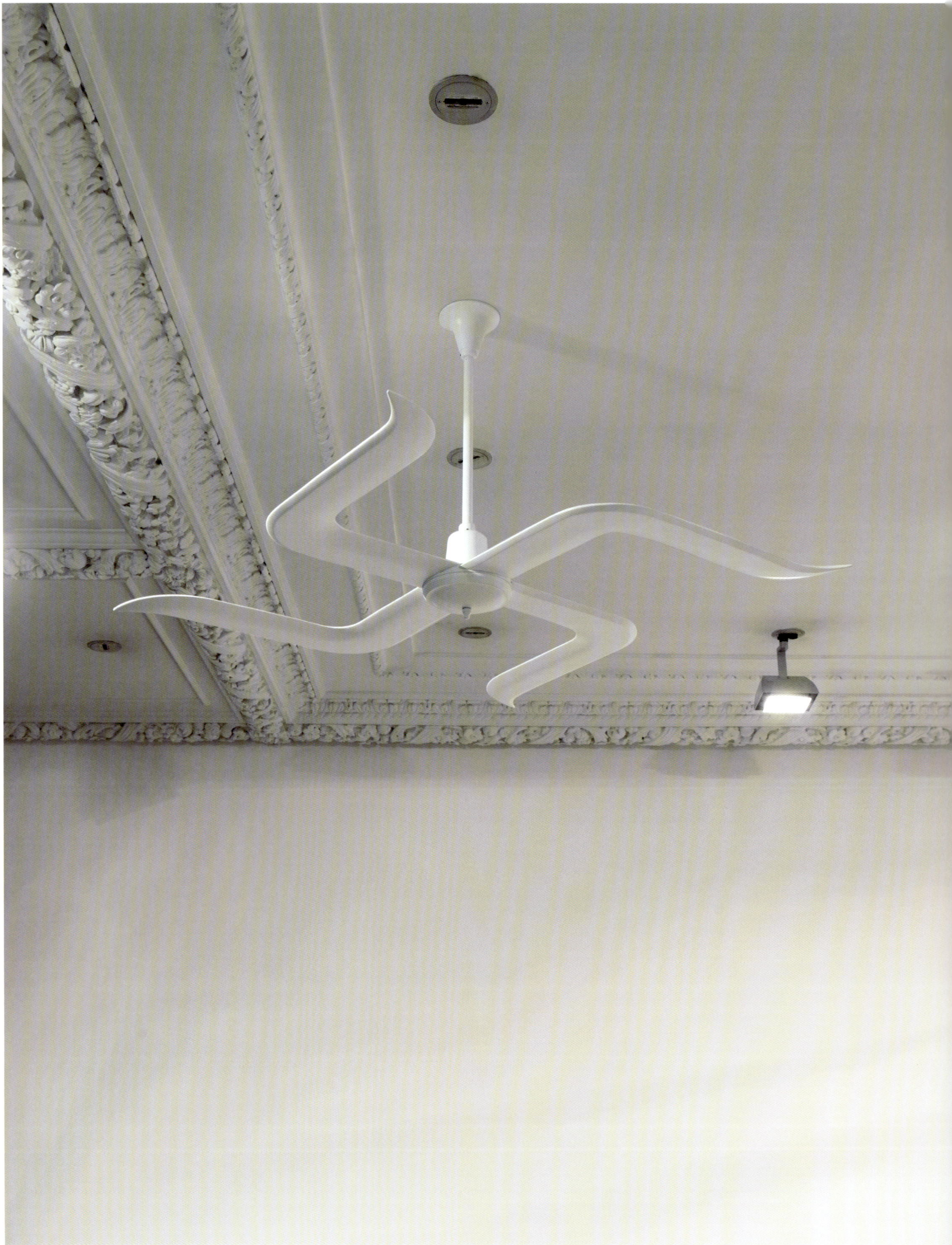

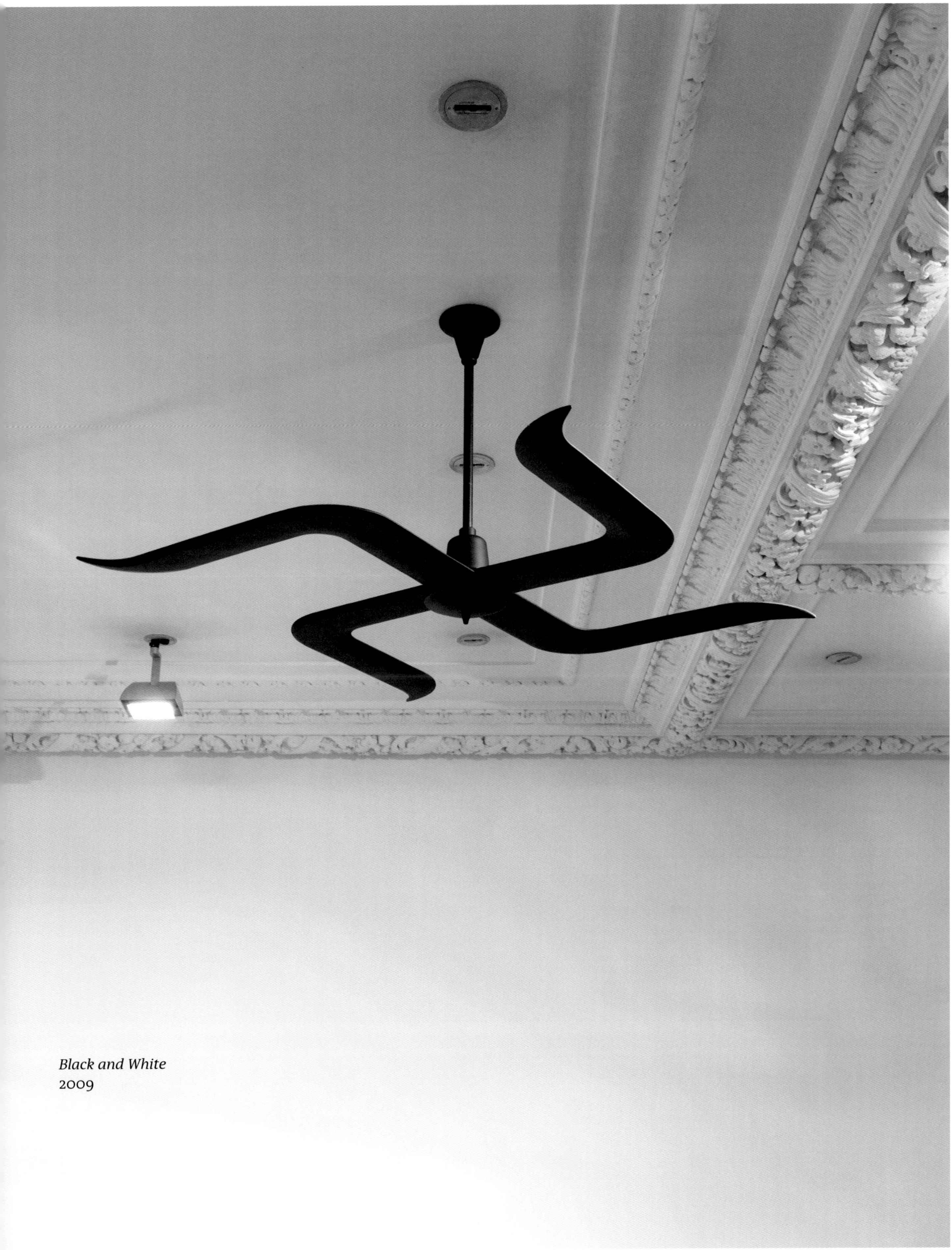

Black and White
2009

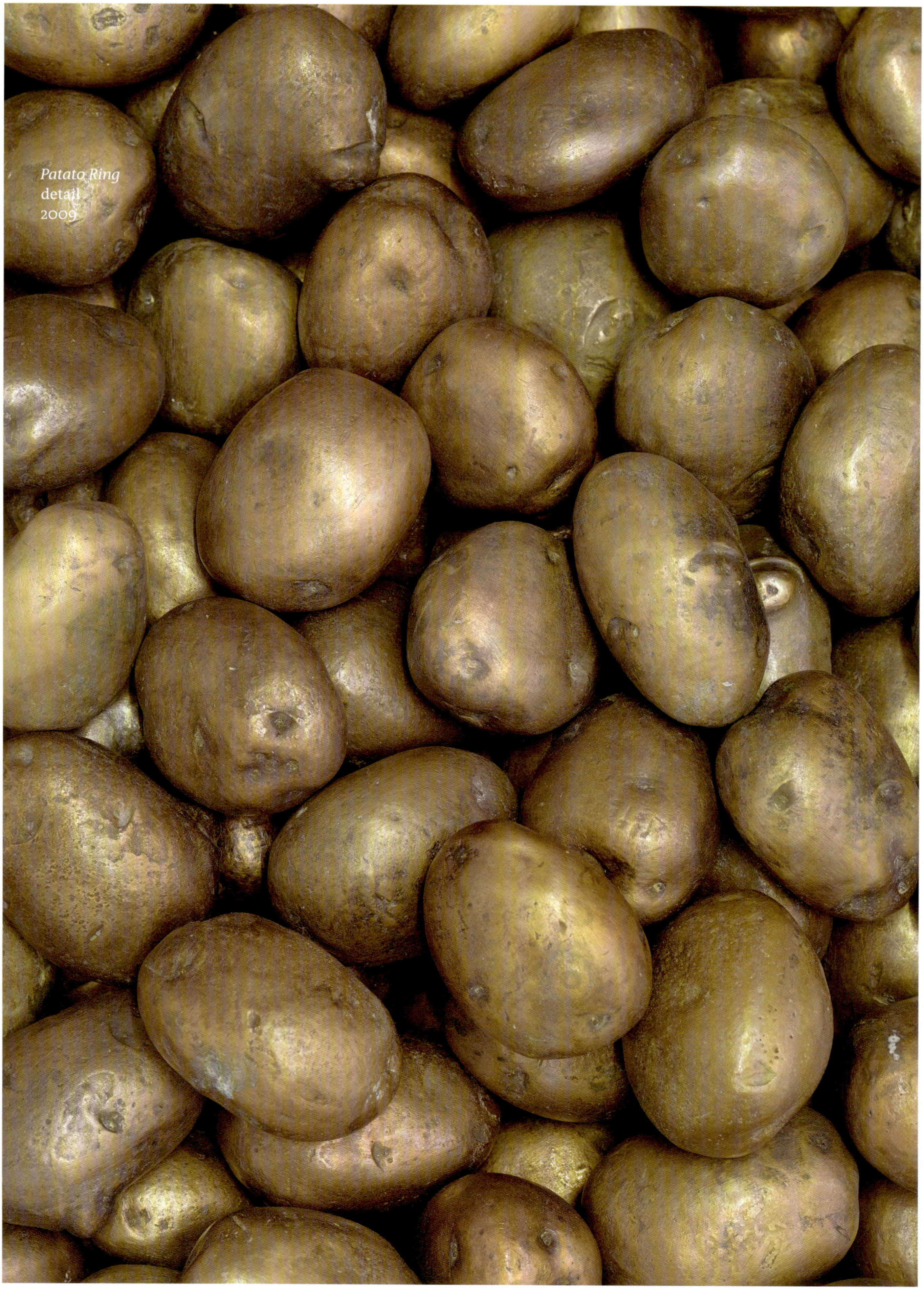

Patato Ring
detail
2009

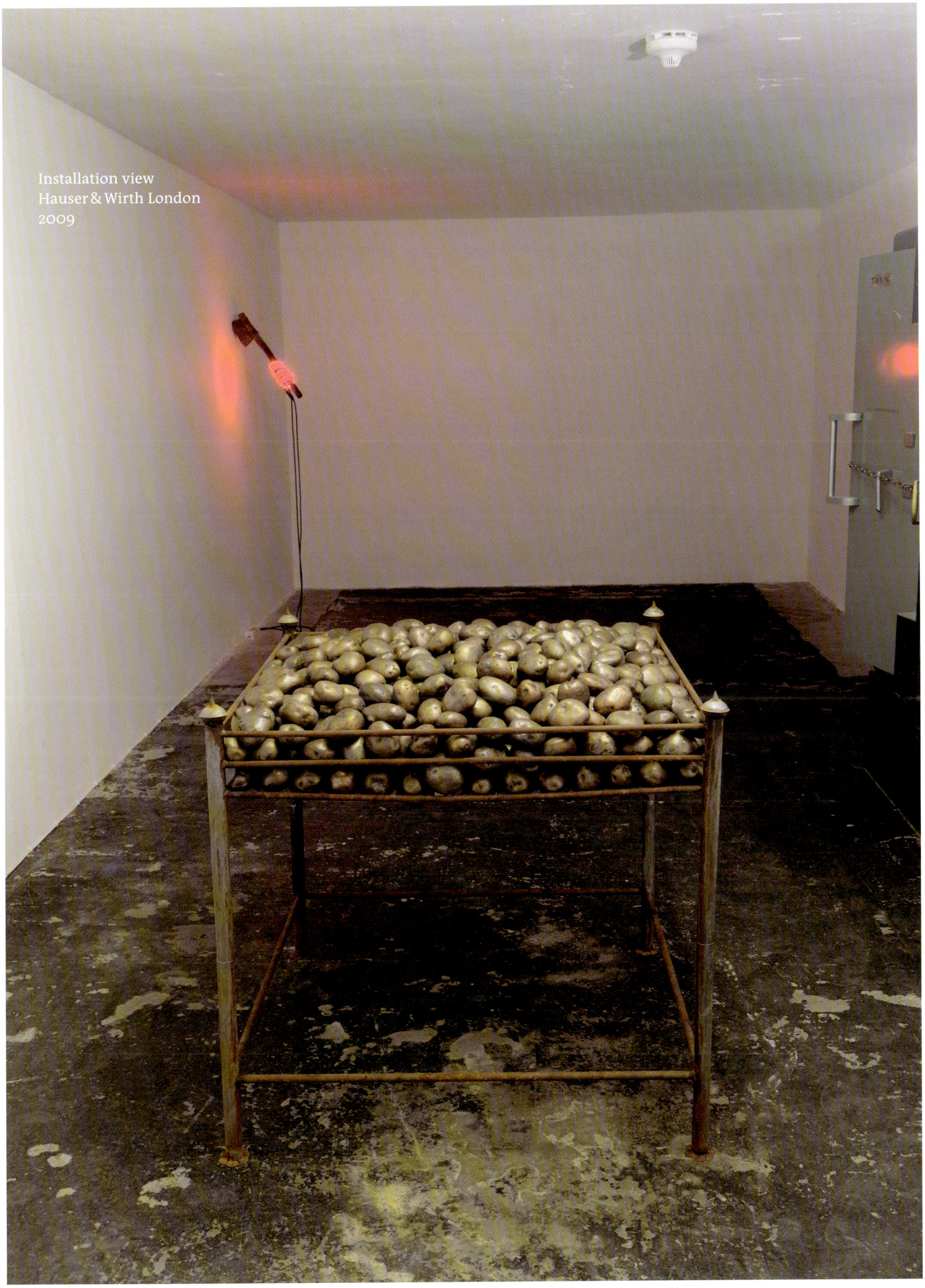
Installation view
Hauser & Wirth London
2009

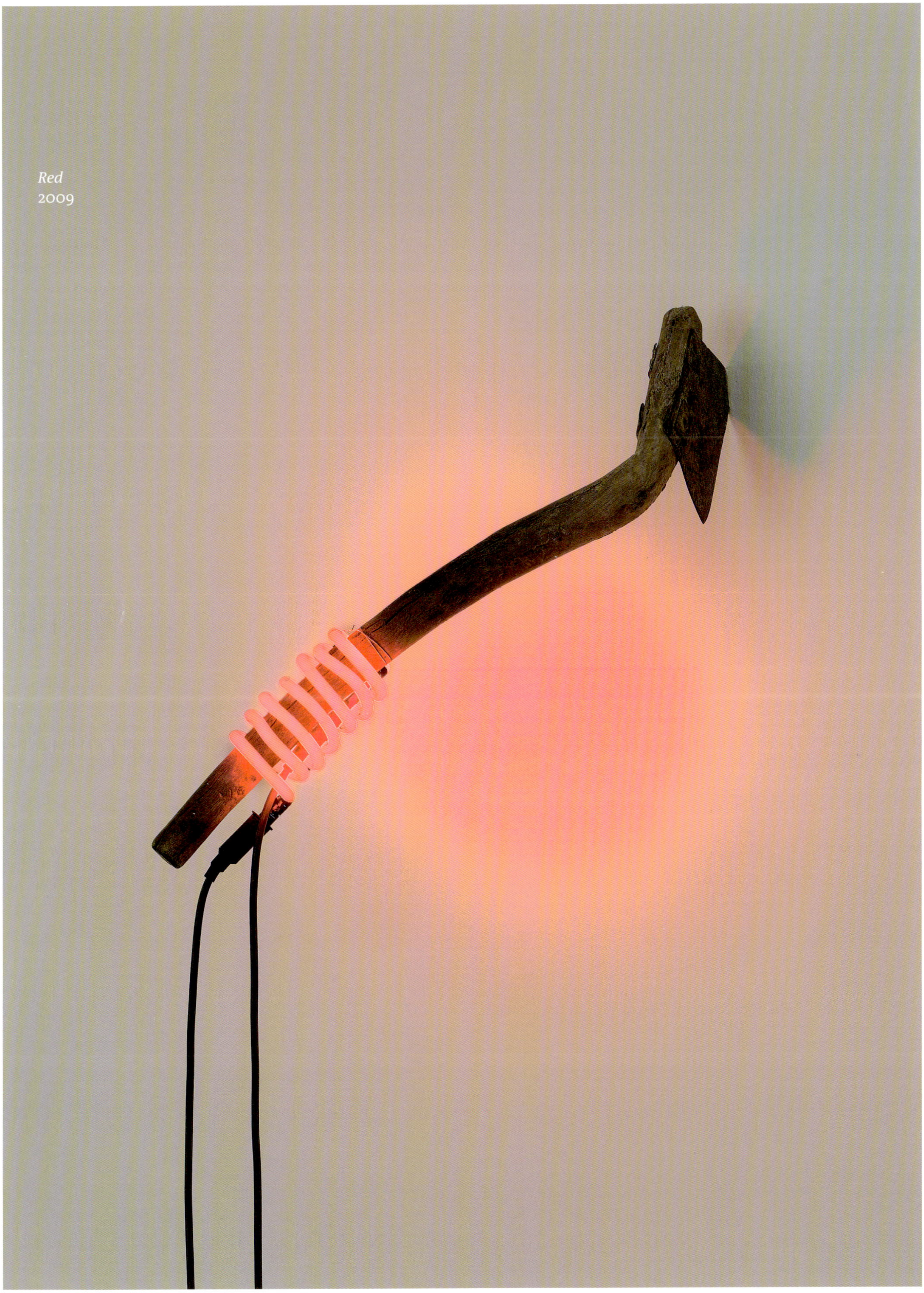

Red
2009

2, 6/7, 31
Aam Aadmi
2009
Painted bronze mangoes in hay, wooden crate on wood and iron table
82.5 × 85 × 48 cm / 32 ½ × 33 ½ × 18⅞ in.

18–21
Jeff the Koons
2009
Painted aluminium
50 boxes, each 52 × 48.5 × 33 cm / 20 ½ × 19 ⅛ × 13 in.

23–26
Et tu, Duchamp?
2009
Black bronze
114 × 88 × 59 cm / 44⅞ × 34⅝ × 23 ¼ in.
Marble plinth
123 × 123 × 122 cm / 48 ⅜ × 48 ⅜ × 48 in.

28
Et tu, Duchamp?
2009
Black bronze
22.9 × 19 × 14 cm / 9 × 7 ½ × 5 ½ in.

33–51
Master Bet
2009
Watercolour body print on handmade paper
29 parts, each 29.7 × 42 cm / 11 ¾ × 16 ½ in.

52–57
Everyday
2009
Stainless steel, stainless steel utensils
Diameter: 213.3 cm / 84 in.
Marble plinth
55 × 240 × 240 cm / 25⅝ × 94 ½ × 94 ½ in.

58–61
A Penny for Belief II
2009
Stainless steel, oil, coins
Diameter: 213.3 cm / 84 in.
Marble plinth
55 × 240 × 240 cm / 25⅝ × 94 ½ × 94 ½ in.

62–65
I believe you
2009
Stainless steel, sandals
Diameter: 213.3 cm / 84 in.
Marble plinth
55 × 240 × 240 cm / 25⅝ × 94 ½ × 94 ½ in.

66–71
Wall
2009
Fibreglass, paint, brick wall
475 × 190.5 × 143.2 cm / 187 × 75 × 56 ⅜ in.

73–75
Spooning
2009
Stainless steel
2 parts
34 × 275 × 52 cm / 13 ⅜ × 108 ¼ × 20 ½ in.

76/77
Black and White
2009
Metal, polystyrene
2 parts
Diameter: each 130 cm / 51 ⅛ in.
Length of pole variable

78/79
Potato Ring
2009
697 bronze potatoes, metal stand
96 × 90.8 × 90.8 cm / 37 ¾ × 35 ¾ × 35 ¾ in.

81
Red
2009
Old axe, neon
Length: 60 cm / 23⅝ in.

Subodh Gupta

1964 born in Khagaul, Bihar, India
Lives and works in New Delhi

Self Portrait, 2010

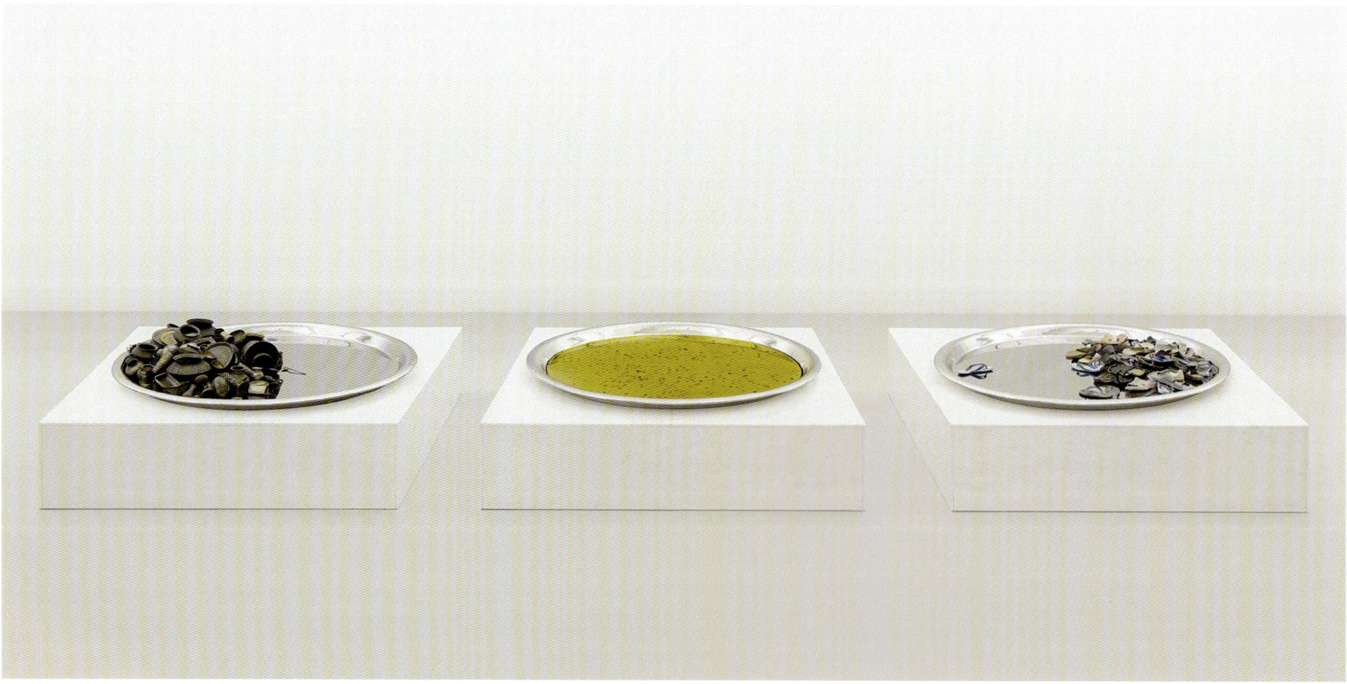

Selected Solo Exhibitions (since 2000)

2010

Hauser & Wirth, Zurich
KÖR at Kunsthalle Wien project space Karlsplatz, *Et tu, Duchamp?*, Vienna, Austria
Pinchuk Art Centre, *Faith matters*, Kiev, Ukraine
Tramway, *Take off your shoes and wash your hands*, Glasgow, Scotland

2009

Hauser & Wirth, *Common Man* आम आदमी, London

2008

Jack Shainman Gallery, *Still, steal, steel*, New York
Galleria Continua, *There is always cinema*, San Gimignano, Italy
Arario Beijing, *Line of Control*, Beijing, China

2007

In SITU / Fabienne Leclerc, *Idol Thief*, Paris
Bodhi Art, *START. STOP*, Mumbai, India
BALTIC Centre for Contemporary Art, *Silk Route*, Gateshead, England

2006

Nature Morte, *Hungry Gods*, New Delhi

2005

In SITU / Fabienne Leclerc, *I can't translate Jootha*, Paris
Jack Shainman Gallery, *I Go Home Every Single Day*, New York
Sakshi Gallery, *Jootha*, Mumbai, India

2004

The Showroom, *I Go Home Every Single Day*, London

2003

Nature Morte, *Saat Samunder Paar*, New Delhi
Art & Public – Cabinet PH, *This Side is the Other Side*, Geneva, Switzerland

2000

Nature Morte, *Recent Works*, New Delhi

Selected Group Exhibitions (since 2000)

2010

Galleria Continua, *REM(A)INDERS*, Beijing, China
Guggenheim Museum, *Contemplating the Void: Interventions in the Guggenheim Museum*, New York
Maillol Museum, *Vanities from Caravaggio to Damien Hirst*, Paris
Herning Kunstmuseum, *Indian Highway*, Herning, Denmark (travelling exhibition)
The Saatchi Gallery, *The Empire Strikes Back: Indian Art Today*, London
S.M.A.K. – Stedelijk Museum voor Actuele Kunst, *Hareng Saur: Ensor and Contemporary Art*, Ghent, Belgium
Reykjavik Art Museum, *Indian Highway*, Reykjavik, Iceland (travelling exhibition)
Tri Postal, *Lille3000: The Silk Road. Saatchi Gallery London in Lille*, Lille, France

2009

Tate Britain, *Altermodern: Tate Triennial 2009*, London
The Garage Centre for Contemporary Culture in Moscow, *Un certain état du monde? Works from the Pinault Collection*, Moscow
Initial Access, *Passage to India Part II*, Wolverhampton, England
Palais des Arts de Dinard, *Who's Afraid of the Artists? A Selection of Works from the Pinault Collection*, Dinard, France
The New Art Gallery Walsall, *Re-imagining Asia. A Thousand Years of Separation*, Walsall, England (travelling exhibition)
Fukuoka Asian Art Museum, *The 4th Fukuoka Asian Art Triennial*, Fukuoka, Japan
Essl Museum, *Chalo! India: A New Era of Indian Art*, Klosterneuburg, Austria (travelling exhibition)
Astrup Fearnley Museum, *Indian Highway*, Oslo, Norway (travelling exhibition)
National Museum of Contemporary Art, *Chalo! India: A New Era of Indian Art*, Seoul, South Korea (travelling exhibition)

2008

Park de Oude Warande & Museum De Pont, *Lustwarande 08 – Wanderland. 3rd Edition Lustwarande*, Tilburg, Netherlands
Villa Manin, *God & Goods – Spirituality and Mass Confusion*, Udine, Italy
Haus der Kulturen der Welt, *Re-imagining Asia. A Thousand Years of Separation*, Berlin (travelling exhibition)
Frank Cohen Collection at Initial Access, *Passage to India*, Wolverhampton, England
Espace Claude Berri, *Indian Focus. Artistes Indiens Contemporains dans la Collection de Claude Berri*, Paris
Mori Art Museum, *Chalo! India: A New Era of Indian Art*, Tokyo (travelling exhibition)
Serpentine Gallery, *Indian Highway*, London (travelling exhibition)
Barbican Art Gallery, *Martian Museum of Terrestrial Art*, London
Devi Art Foundation, *Where in the World*, New Delhi
Kunsthalle zu Kiel, *Heavy Metal. On the Inexplicable Lightness of a Material*, Kiel, Germany
48ºC Public. Art. Ecology, New Delhi
Institut Valencia d'Art Modern, *India Moderna*, Valencia, Spain

2007

Hangar Bicocca, *Urban Manners – 15 Contemporary Artists from India*, Milan
Art Gallery of Ontario, *Hungry God*, Toronto
The Newark Museum, *India: Public Places / Private Spaces*, Newark, New Jersey
Domaine Pommery, *L'Emprise du lieu – L'expérience Pommery #4*, Reims, France
Sammlung Daimler Chrysler – Lekha and Anupam Poddar Collections, *Private / Corporate IV*, Berlin
Palazzo Grassi, *Sequence 1. Painting & Sculpture from the François Pinault Collection*, Venice

2006

P.S.1 MoMA, *Altered, Stitched and Gathered*, New York
Taipei Biennial 2006, Taipei, Taiwan
Istanbul Modern, *Venice – Istanbul*, Istanbul, Turkey
Palais des Beaux-Arts de Bruxelles, *Contemporary India*, Brussels, Belgium
Église St-Bernard et vitrine de la Galerie In SITU, *Nuit Blanche*, Paris
Lille 3000, *Bombaysers de Lille*, Lille, France
Arario Gallery, *Hungry Gods*, Beijing, China
Galerie Enrico Navarra, Plage de Pampelonne, *Made by Indians. Art on the Beach #5*, Commune de Ramatuelle, France
The Showroom, *If it didn't exist you'd have to invent it*, London

2005

Krannert Art Museum, *Balance and Power: Performance and Surveillance in Video Art*, Champaign, Illinois
La Biennale di Venezia, *Always a Little Further*, Venice
Museum of Contemporary Art, *Universal Experience: Art, Life and the Tourist's Eye*, Chicago, Illinois (travelling exhibition)
Hayward Gallery, *Universal Experience: Art, Life and the Tourist's Eye*, London (travelling exhibition)
The Herzliya Museum of Contemporary Art, *Weightless Space*, Herzliya, Israel
The Moscow Biennale of Contemporary Art, *Dialectics of Hope*, Moscow
École nationale supérieure des Beaux-Arts, *Indian Summer*, Paris

2004

Fukuoka Asian Art Museum, *Indian Video Art: History in Motion*, Fukuoka, Japan
Centre A – Vancouver International Centre for Contemporary Art, *Two-Man Show*, Vancouver, Canada
Sakshi Gallery, *Vanitas Vanitatum*, Mumbai

2003

8. Biennale Havanna, Cuba
Haus der Kulturen der Welt, *Body. City. Citing Contemporary Culture in India*, Berlin
Henie Onstad Kunstsenter, *The Tree from the Seed, Contemporary Art from India*, Høvikodden, Norway

2002

Busan Metropolitan Art Museum, Busan Biennale, Korea
IMA – Institute of Modern Art, *Self: Contemporary Indian Video Art*, Brisbane, Australia
Manchester City Art Gallery, *Indian Art: Home-Street-Shrine-Bazaar-Museum*, Manchester, England
Kunsthalle Wien, *Kapital & Karma*, Vienna, Austria
Palais de Tokyo, *Inaugural Show*, Paris
India Habitat Centre, *Sidewinder*, New Delhi (travelling exhibition)

2001

Galleria Continua, *Post Production (Sampling, Programming & Displaying)*, San Gimignano, Italy
Museum of Fine Art, *Context as Content – Museum as Metaphor*, Chandigarh, India (travelling exhibition)

2000

Asian Section of the Kwangju Biennale 2000, *Invisible Boundary: Metamorphosed Asian Art*, Kwangju, Korea (travelling exhibition)
Niigata City Prefectural Civil Centre Gallery, *Invisible Boundary: Metamorphosed Asian Art*, Niigata, Japan (travelling exhibition)
Utsunomiya Museum of Art, *Invisible Boundary: Metamorphosed Asian Art*, Utsunomiya, Japan (travelling exhibition)
CRAC Alsace – Centre Rhénan d'Art Contemporain, *Négotiations*, Sète, France

Credits & Copyrights

Front Cover
Subodh Gupta, *Et tu, Duchamp?*, 2009
Frontispiece
Subodh Gupta, *Aam Aadmi*, 2009 (detail)

Photo Credits
Mike Bruce (pp. 2, 6/7, 16, 18–31, 50–81); Subodh Gupta (p. 8); Stefan Altenburger (pp. 10, 14, 84); Katalin Deér (p. 12/on the left); Lorenza Mercuri (p. 13); Rebecca Fanuele (p. 15); Ananjay Bushan (p. 17); Barbora Gerny (pp. 33–48)

All works of the artist courtesy of Hauser & Wirth, except pp. 13, 15: In SITU, Fabienne Leclerc, Paris

Imprint

Published by
Hauser & Wirth
196A Piccadilly
UK-London W1J 9DY
T +44 (0)207 287 23 00
F +44 (0)207 287 66 00
E london@hauserwirth.com
www.hauserwirth.com
In Co-edition with
JRP | Ringier
Letzigraben 134
CH-8047 Zurich
T +41 (0)43 311 27 50
F +41 (0)43 311 27 51
E info@jrp-ringier.com
www.jrp-ringier.com

JRP | Ringier books are available internationally at selected bookstores and from the following distribution partners:

Switzerland
Buch 2000,
AVA Verlagsauslieferung AG,
Centralweg 16, CH-8910 Affoltern a.A.,
buch2000@ava.ch, www.ava.ch
France
Les presses du réel, 35 rue Colson,
F-21000 Dijon,
info@lespressesdureel.com,
www.lespressesdureel.com
Germany and Austria
Vice Versa Vertrieb,
Immanuelkirchstraße 12,
D-10405 Berlin,
info@vice-versa-vertrieb.de,
www.vice-versa-vertrieb.de
UK and other European countries
Cornerhouse Publications,
70 Oxford Street,
UK-Manchester M1 5NH,
publications@cornerhouse.org,
www.cornerhouse.org/books
USA, Canada, Asia, and Australia
D.A.P./Distributed Art Publishers,
155 Sixth Avenue, 2nd Floor,
USA-New York, NY 10013,
dap@dapinc.com, www.artbook.com

For a list of our partner bookshops or for any general questions, please contact JRP | Ringier directly at info@jrp-ringier.com, or visit our homepage www.jrp-ringier.com for further information about our program.

This book was published on occasion of the exhibition *Subodh Gupta – Common Man* आम आदमी at Hauser & Wirth London, 1–31 October 2009

Editor
Sara Harrison
Editorial Coordination
Michaela Unterdörfer
Copy Editing
Flora Boillot, Julia Lenz, Michaela Unterdörfer
Proofreading
Louise Stein
Transcription
Almut Dhraif
Typography
Istvàn Scheibler, Sebastian Fessel, Berlin
Colour Separation and Print
Musumeci S.p.A., Quart (Aosta)

Printed in Europe

ISBN 978-3-03764-143-9